Larry ~~~~~~ Guide to

Central Florida
Bass Waters

by Larry Larsen

Book II in the Bass Waters Series
by Larsen's Outdoor Publishing

Copyright (c) 1991 by Larry Larsen

Please note that factual contact information, persons, addresses and telephone numbers listed in this book are subject to change. In the course of time, state-wide regulations may change. So may management policies on individual lakes and ponds. Launch sites, marinas, guides and lake sizes may even change unexpectedly. It is prudent for the reader to check current fisheries laws, regulations, restrictions and other data regarding all water bodies prior to fishing them.

ISBN 0-936513-19-5

Library of Congress 91-76768

Published by:

LARSEN'S OUTDOOR PUBLISHING
2640 Elizabeth Place
Lakeland, FL 33813

PRINTED IN THE UNITED STATES OF AMERICA

1 2 3 4 5 6 7 8 9 10

ACKNOWLEDGMENTS

I want to thank the many guides of Central Florida that I have fished with over the past 24 years. Their sharing of knowledge regarding the region's lakes and rivers have helped in this effort. I also am grateful for my avid bass fishing friends, those anglers in the Florida Outdoor Writers Association and others who shared a boat with me on most of the waters mentioned in this book.

Thanks go to Frank Sargeant, Jim Bitter, Bing McClellan, Doug Gilley, Ken Daubert, Max Braynon, Dan Thurmond, Bob Stonewater and all my friends in the media, the newspaper and magazine columnists and the editors who are interested in sharing with their readers information about my entire line of outdoor books. I appreciate their kind comments.

Special thanks go to my wife, Lilliam. Her valuable contribution in reviewing, design layout and production assistance to develop **Larry Larsen's Guide To Central Florida Bass Waters** is much appreciated. So are the great maps that illustrate many of the chapters which were provided by my good friend Bob Knops of Fishing Hot Spots.

PREFACE

If you want to learn more about your favorite water, or learn about other overlooked hotspots in this region, this Guide is for you.

If your favorite water is not mentioned, there could be several reasons:

1. The author is not aware of the productivity of your favorite spot;

2. With so many waters to cover, it is impossible to mention each and every one;

3. The author may be keeping it a secret for himself.

This book should be a reference source for all anglers who fish or wish to fish in the future the waters of Central Florida. Each chapter focuses on the "name" lakes and rivers in the region that almost always produce good bass fishing and on many overlooked waters that quietly produce good bass fishing as well. The places mentioned in each chapter are waters where you can usually catch largemouth bass. Those waters where sunshine (hybrid striped bass) and striped bass are available are also noted.

Additionally, productive methods that will help the reader catch more and larger bass on these waters are presented in Larry Larsen's Guide To Central Florida Bass Waters. The proven techniques, lures and baits discussed within the pages of this book should help you be better prepared to tackle one of the rivers or lakes in the book on your next time out.

CONTENTS

The author has extensively covered the region's bass waters to research magazine articles and books. He has caught several hundred bass from 5 to 12 pounds from Florida lakes and rivers.

INTRODUCTION

THE GUIDE AND YOUR GUIDE

Learn everything there is to know about your next Central Florida bass fishing destination and your trip will be better planned and more productive. **Guide To Central Florida Bass Waters** is your best resource for trip planning, seasonal information, water characteristics and other interesting and necessary details that will make your bass fishing trip less of a guessing game.

Guide To Central Florida Bass Waters focuses on the top bass rivers and lakes from Tampa and Orlando to Palatka. This region is very productive for big largemouth!

While fishing pressure is more focused on Central Florida than on waters in the other two Florida regions, it is spread out over more water in terms of diversity and geographic coverage. This region's waters are the state's most popular for a reason. They produce lots of bass and offer beautiful scenery at the same time.

To help you better locate productive spots, the book lists specific locations on each of the waters covered, and effective techniques that the author and other expert bass guides and professional fishermen have employed. Launching areas, maps and other lake details are also included for many of the region's lakes and rivers.

Largemouth bass are the main focus of this book, yet striped bass and hybrid striper bass (sunshine bass) are also mentioned when the opportunity exists for a significant catch on a specific body of water. Information on lake records is included, for those anglers wishing to prepare in advance to try to set their own.

The specific waters within these pages were picked because they are consistently productive for numbers or bass, and/or because they produce lunker-size largemouth. These waters are also popular, with a local reputation for quality fisheries, and are accessible to most anglers with canoes, johnboats or larger bass boats. If your favorite lake or river isn't mentioned, it may be because it's too small and heavy fishing pressure could devastate it, or because it's private, or because it's currently not known to be productive. Finally, it may simply be located in a different region, so check the other books in this series.

Some of the most interesting and valuable aspects of **Guide to Central Florida Bass Waters** are the seasonal information, lures and tackle recommendations, and detailed locations mentioned for improving the angler's bass catching success. The author, Larry Larsen, takes the time to outline specific locations in lakes, rivers and creeks, information that is normally not possible to include in many magazine articles due to lack of space. It is certain that the reader will learn much new information revealed in this book for the first time.

For the past 24 years, Larry has covered the state in his quest for great bass waters...from the sand hill ponds in Holmes and Walton Counties to Titusville's Merritt Island Refuge, from the St. Mary's River at the Georgia line to the brackish canals in the Everglades. Fishing more than 1,000 of Florida's lakes and rivers qualify him to author the Guide to Florida Bass Waters series of books.

It is improbable at least that readers would not learn something from Larry's knowledge and experience. An award-winning author of over a dozen other books on bass fishing, few writers are more qualified and knowledgeable about Florida's bass waters. He enjoys Florida bass fishing as much as he enjoys writing about it, and he's as good an angler as he is a writer.

His Florida fishing success includes numerous bass between five and 12 pounds from the waters mentioned. He also held a line-class world record for Suwannee bass. His expertise in developing successful patterns for both artificial and live bait fishing has resulted in extensive recording of his catches and successes through several thousand color slides and magazine articles.

Over the past eight years, Larry has covered the state for Outdoor Life as their Florida Editor, fishing and writing about the top waters and those often overlooked. His numerous articles on Florida bass waters have also appeared in Florida Sportsman, and many other regional and national publications. He is a member of the Outdoor Writers Association of America (OWAA), the Southeastern Outdoor Press Association (SEOPA), and the Florida Outdoor Writers Association (FOWA).

Guide to Central Florida Bass Waters is the second of the Bass Waters Series which also includes North Florida, and soon will include South Florida Bass Waters.

Guide to Central Florida Bass Waters includes several appendices that an informed reader should find of interest. Appendix A lists the significant lakes and rivers in each Central Florida county and the surface acreage of each. The addresses and telephone numbers of the game and fish office and those of the county chambers of commerce are listed in Appendix B.

To help broaden your knowledge on bass fishing, inshore fishing and hunting for deer and turkey, Appendix C is the informative Fishing & Hunting Resource Directory. A compilation of quality outdoor reference books that are extremely popular with sportsmen is presented. For example, Larry's award-winning nine-book BASS SERIES LIBRARY details highly productive fish catching methods and special techniques. Other books published by Larsen's Outdoor Publishing reveal how to be more productive on your next fishing or hunting trip. This additional information in the Resource Directory will help you catch more bass and inshore fish, and locate more deer and turkey on your next hunting. They will help make you more successful!

Information on how to obtain the most comprehensive maps for many of the state's lakes is also available in Appendix D.

Finally, the comprehensive Index includes a cross reference of lakes, cities, bass species, counties and fisheries information that will help you quickly locate and review each reference throughout the book.

I'm sure you will enjoy learning from Larry's expertise, as I have over the years. -- Lilliam M. Larsen

1

REBOUNDING RODMAN RESERVOIR

THE NEWS WAS BLEAK. The headlines screamed, "Major Fish Kill Wipes Out Rodman!," and "Rodman Reservoir Is Dead!" The obituaries were written in late 1985 and early 1986. It was gloom and doom, and the fishery that was reportedly depleted would not regain its strength until maybe the mid-90s.

But the reporters and many others more recognized as experts were wrong. The premature death announcements for the Corps of Engineers' impoundment stemmed from an apparent chemical runoff upstream in the Oklawaha River. It entered the lake and forced many fish to the dam, where low oxygen killed a large number of them.

An estimated eight million fish perished during September, and about 50 percent were gamefish. A biologist reported largemouth bass up to 12 pounds stacked a foot deep along the shoreline after the kill. Most reports predicted that it would take several years to rebuild the bass population of Rodman. Numerous articles in newspapers and magazines convinced anglers that the fishing here was ruined.

This bass fishery was out of action a few months in the mid 1980s, but today it yields huge bass.

Gainesville resident, Shaw Grigsby, didn't quit fishing the lake when the news hit, however. And he claims that bass fishing ever since has been fantastic. In his frequent visits to Rodman after the big kill, he noticed very few other anglers on the lake. Grigsby found, though, that the big kill didn't eliminate all of the bass. On the contrary, many were left, and he found them to be healthy and hungry.

The young angler, who has been justifiably impressed with the quantity and quality of bass in the impoundment, likes to toss baits in the areas that lie between Kenwood and Orange Springs Landings. There is more diverse cover in that area, the "center section" of Rodman Reservoir.

"One of the largest concentrations of largemouth exist in the standing timber, vegetation mats, old creek channels, and major river channel," says Grigsby. "Upstream, are only the Orange Springs flats and the Oklawaha. Toward the dam, is a large expanse of flats."

Grisgby, who has caught Rodman bass of up to 11 3/4 pounds on a buzz bait, usually opts for topwater lures. He'll use them most of the year, particularly from February through November. When not tossing a buzz bait, he'll use either an injured-minnow type lure, or a tiny Torpedo surface plug.

Most of my Rodman catches have occurred in either shallow or mid-depth waters. A crankbait is often my choice for an area just out from the dam where the old Oklawaha River channel makes a bend. Large, deep-running plugs, as well as vibrating plugs have been productive there. I've caught big bass by flippin' worms in the floating water cabbage around the old river channel. There are other kinds of areas on the lake that also draw my attention.

Rodman is not typical Florida water. Its variety of structure and depth is unparalleled in this state. There's plenty of vegetation and shallow flats, plus an abundance of submerged stumps and timber, creek channels, drops, humps and banks. The reservoir also has numerous natural springs and artesian wells that flow into it. That makes for a water temperature that is pretty consistent in some areas and productive bass fishing, even in the coldest winter.

FLUCTUATIONS IN WATER LEVEL AND SUCCESS

Rodman's fishing has been up and down, thanks in part to drawdowns. The reservoir, located in the middle of the Ocala National Forest, experienced several drawdowns in the interest of aquatic weed control during the late 1970's. Bass were very accessible to anglers and fishing pressure increased significantly when the Rodman Pool water level was minimal and the bass pickings relatively easy. The fishery suffered.

Lunker-size largemouth were scarce in the lake during the late 70's. Numerous mid-range bass were taken from the lake, but not even the profuse vegetation could protect the fishery. Much of

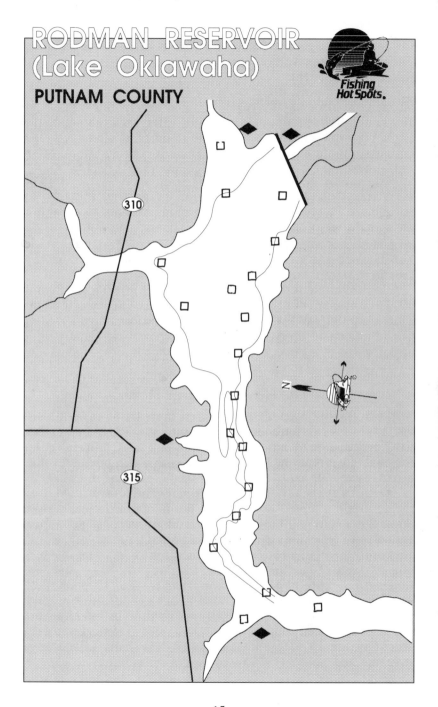

RODMAN RESERVOIR
(Lake Oklawaha)
PUTNAM COUNTY

310

315

that was lying high and dry for a period of three or four months. The lunker resource could not quickly recover from the bass fishermen onslaught.

The drawdowns, while normally employed as a very positive means to control aquatic vegetation and benefit the fishery, can also be too frequent on some bodies of water. The characteristics of the reservoir and its most valuable resource, in Rodman's case, big bass, should have received paramount consideration. Many lunker bass guides on these waters believe that they didn't.

The initial drawdown on Rodman didn't occur until 1975. Prior to that, the reservoir was renown for lunker bass. Constructed in 1969 as part of the now defunct Cross Florida Barge Canal project, the controversial waters soon established a reputation for largemouth of huge proportions. The twisting Oklawaha River was dammed and a straight 150-foot wide canal dredged nearby, creating some 16 miles of superior bass habitat.

Continuation of the 107-mile-long canal project was halted in 1971 due primarily to environmental concerns, particularly on the Florida aquifer, and to the decreasing financial feasibility. Flooding of the hardwood forest gave Florida anglers a new and unique opportunity, though: an artificial impoundment with a tremendous habitat for freshwater game fish and their forage.

THE HISTORICAL HEY DAYS

I certainly enjoyed the great fishing there in the early 70's and caught several bass between five and 10 pounds. The most powerful fish I ever had on hit a large crankbait like a "freight train" going the opposite direction. It burned drag until my 25-pound test line broke. I can only assume that it was the "Mother of all Lunkers!"

With an abundance of standing timber and forage-filled flats, the reservoir zoomed into angling headlines in the early '70's. Several bass in the 10 to 15-pound category were caught. Local bass club tournaments often found a 10 or 11-pound largemouth anchoring a winning catch, and in a national bass tournament in late 1973, a one-day limit (10 fish) weighing over 60 pounds was weighed in. "Big bass" of that tournament was 12 pounds, 13 ounces.

The crystal clear waters soon allowed an influx of water hyacinth and hydrilla which remain today. The weed growth, essentially absent in the 1973 tournaments when crankbaits gained huge stringers and popularity, caused successful methods to change.

On cloudy days, flippin' around heavy cover in Rodman Reservoir and its tributaries is often productive.

Today, the logs and scattered stumps lie beneath pennywort, dollar weed, hyacinth and water cabbage.

Jigging small leadhead jigs during cool weather became popular. It involved using a garden rake to make a fishing hole in the masses of floating water hyacinths. The 1/16 ounce jigs were dropped through the 'new' openings in the thick cover and bass were there, feeding on the tiny freshwater shrimp, bugs and other forage present. The size of these fish was not always impressive, but a cold zero-day could often be salvaged with the method.

Then, in the late 1970's, hydrilla began to 'take over' the entire reservoir. It rooted in 15 feet of water, choking off areas to anglers, but the bass loved it. Forage was everywhere, making feeding easier, yet anglers unaccustomed to fishing such vegetation-intensive areas were frustrated. Guides and weekend anglers that learned how to cope with the 'problem' continued to do well.

Soon, however, the pressure for annual drawdowns increased and the Army Corps of Engineers complied. Baitfish and bass were concentrated in the open water then, making them too vulnerable. Lack of drawdowns during the early 1980's helped to increase productivity, and guides are happy with that.

TODAY'S TROPHY BASS FISHING

Guide Dan Thurmond, who fishes Rodman almost daily with huge shiners, is in agreement that the bass fishing is great. He is an avid proponent of catch and release and a critic of those anglers who keep more lunkers than they wish to mount. Rodman is once again hot, he contends.

My wife, Lilliam, and I traveled to the lake to fish with Dan one June and to check out the fishery. Lilliam, looking for a "birthday" bass, caught one of her largest ever, a healthy seven pounder. Like an 8-1/2 pounder she caught earlier, she released it. We took seven largemouth, including two others over five pounds, in just over five hours of fishing on her birthday.

Thurmond's largest client-caught bass from Rodman before the kill was taken by Miami resident, Charlie Haag. He was using ten-inch river shiners near a hydrilla-clogged weed bed when the fish hit and buried itself in a mass of weed. The huge bass was 29 1/2 inches long with a 21 1/4 inch girth and weighed 14 pounds.

Less than two months after the big kill a Thurmond party caught two bass that each weighed over 11 pounds. About nine months after the "fish slaughter," a Thurmond client caught a 15 pound, 3 ounce largemouth from Rodman. Numerous ten-pound-plus bass have been caught and released by Thurmond and clients in the six years since. That activity, while impressive, is an increasingly frequent occurrence today on Rodman, or Lake Oklawaha, as it's known to map makers.

Some Rodman bass have even been more impressive. Dan Harris, of Interlachen, Florida was fishing with his wife on the flats one morning when something unusual happened. They had caught a couple of five pound bass in two hours, when Dan's shiner became nervous. The bass sucked the shiner under, and Dan set the hook. He quickly played the bass to the boat and landed the unusual fish.

"What is it?", his wife asked.

18

It was a largemouth bass that was completely orange in color! The fish weighed 5 pounds, 12 ounces and was 25 1/2 inches in length. The oddity was kept at the National Fish Hatchery aquarium in Welaka, Florida for several days before it died. Hatchery supervisor, Jim Maxwell, verified the catch but could not offer any explanation for the unusual coloration, other than it being just a freak of nature.

Large Rodman bass of normal coloration can be taken in deep water without the aid of a depth finder. During the summer and fall, the hydrilla defines many deep holes and creek channels. Big bass will work the edges. Best times to catch behemoth bass here are the winter months, but the period of April through June, and again from August through December are also peak times.

WHERE TO LOOK

Some of the better areas in the main pool to fish are at the junction of Deep Creek and the Oklawaha River channel which drops from eight feet down to 25, the hydrilla beds and stumps in front of the dam, and the stumpy flat area south of the Oklawaha River channel nearer shore. Hangups are a reality in the pool area, but many bass are taken there year around.

Hydrilla edges adjacent to 15 feet of water along the Barge Canal spoil banks, and those cuts through the spoil banks and weedbeds usually provide good bass fishing, particularly when the locks are letting water out of the impoundment. Bass gather on the canal side in the hydrilla and other vegetation and wait for forage. The points of the spoil islands are very productive, especially during high winds, wave action and overcast cloud cover.

Bass in the seven to nine foot deep flats off Deep Creek often hang out around the channel as it winds through the area. Anywhere the Oklawaha River channel crosses the barge canal also provides an excellent big bass area. The area depths will range from 15 to 20 feet. The Oklawaha River channel cuts through the flats north of the barge canal spoil humps, and bass set up home at the edge of the 15 to 20 foot deep channel.

Largemouth are often found in the bends and horseshoe turns of the Oklawaha River channel as it crosses the barge canal and winds through the flooded forest off the pool area. The channel provides some unique structure and topographical changes. The bass typically hold on the outer bends of the channel. The best areas are usually the sharpest turns in 5 to 8 feet of water. Anytime the channel leaves the treeline and floating surface canopy, anglers with sonar units have a chance to thoroughly fish an outer bend.

Specifically, the bends of the wood-surrounded river channel near the Blue Springs Cut entrance are productive bass areas. Blue Springs is one of the larger springs on Rodman and reached via a cut through the timber flats south of the river channel. The flow is not very noticeable, but the area holds fish. The nearby area known as Doctor's Cove is a productive bass hole behind the standing dead timber and floating canopies.

TACTICS, LURES & BAIT

Live bait now accounts for the majority of huge bass on these waters. Native shiners seven to 12-inch long are frequently drifted on a cork set three or four feet above the baitfish. A 5/0 or 6/0 hook through both lips is often the only shiner adornment that I use when after trophies. I'll fish them in areas with river or wind current for best results. If the water depth is more than 10 feet, I'll usually remove the bobber.

During a cold front, bass will often move deeper into the cover, calling for more effort on the part of the angler to get a bait to them. Fishing shiners on a tight line without weight or bobber will allow the baitfish to penetrate the floating vegetation easier and result in more strikes. Another way to locate bass during frontal conditions is to move the boat into the vegetation canopy and scoop a "hole" in the weeds. Then, drop a shiner through the opening and let it swim several feet.

Nine to 12-inch plastic worms fished slowly over the aquatic plant life has also been very productive for me. By using minimal weight, the lure will make contact with the edges of the vegetation. I'll opt for a shorter, red- or moccasin-colored wigglers with curly tail under bright skies. Weed Walkers and other snagless artificials can be highly successful in and around the hydrilla patches when the sun is not straight overhead.

Early or late in the day, or during overcast days, lures that resemble injured minnows tossed into open pockets, take their share of monster largemouth also. It's best to work them methodically in a twitch, pause, twitch retrieve. I like to fish such lures around the cuts in the canal berm. When the locks are being operated, a current through such areas is set up, and baitfish gets sucked in and out of them.

The author finds the winter months normally provide the best trophy bass fishing on Rodman.

Buzz baits and other topwater lures worked above the hydrilla in the flats can be productive, particularly from February through November. Wood surface plugs are responsible for many trophy-size bass. A crankbait is often a good choice for the flats area just out from the dam where the submerged Oklawaha River channel makes a bend. Large, deep-running plugs, as well as vibrating plugs, have been productive there.

LAKE DETAILS

The reservoir is 13,000 acres and has a maximum depth of 30 feet, length of 16 miles and width of 3 miles. It has an average depth of 8 feet. Since its construction, the level of the reservoir has been manipulated from approximately 13.2 feet to 18.2 feet. These planned drawdowns in the interest of aquatic weed control, flooded woodland preservation, construction purposes and fisheries management occur periodically.

The section of Rodman, from its headwaters at Eureka Dam to Paynes Landing, is called the riverine section. It consists of flooded woodlands and resembles the pre-impoundment Oklawaha River. The middle section, from Paynes Landing to Orange Springs, consists of dead standing timber and large areas of floating vegetation through which flow the river. The pool section from Orange Springs to the dam includes the river channel, Cross Florida Barge Canal and flats. It consists of expansive areas of floating vegetation, submersed vegetation, dead standing timber and submerged and partially submerged logs and trees.

Three inlets, the Oklawaha River, Deep Creek/Sweetwater Creek and Orange Creek, all drain into the lake, with the Oklawaha being the major source of reservoir water. Numerous underwater springs also contribute slightly. Water levels are maintained by the U.S. Army Corps of Engineers dam. Rodman Dam, located on the east side of the reservoir, controls the lake's water level and flows into the Oklawaha River below. While fluctuations usually do not exceed two feet, drawdowns of five feet have occurred periodically since the mid 70's.

The lake has approximately 90 miles of shoreline and profuse vegetation. Several floating masses of water hyacinth, water lettuce and flooded trees tend to define certain river channels, shallow humps and spring holes. Hydrilla is the dominant submergent-type vegetation. It is found throughout the reservoir and covers 2,800 acres. During late summer and early fall, most of the hydrilla has grown to the surface. Only the deeper areas of the Oklawaha River channel and Barge Canal are generally free of the vegetation.

The floating water hyacinth are primarily confined to areas of flooded timber along the old Oklawaha River channel where they have lodged and along much of the shoreline. The densely-packed mats of floating vegetation in the areas of flooded timber on Rodman also include pennywort and water hemlock.

Launch And Navigation Details

There are no fuel facilities or marinas on the water. The free boat ramps spread around the reservoir help alleviate any problems caused by that, however. On the east side of the lake off highway 19 just south of the Barge Canal is the Rodman Recreation Area. Special regulations include open gate hours of 5 a.m. to 10 p.m. for non-campers. On the north side off highway 315 is the popular Kenwood Recreational Area. On the west side off highway 315 in Orange Springs is the Orange Springs Recreation Area.

Other, less popular (and more remote) ramps include the Paynes Landing area on the southwest side of the lake off highway 315 near Cypress Bayou Fish Camp, and the Hog Valley ramp located off Forest Road 77 on the south side of the reservoir opposite the Orange Springs Recreation Area. On the south side of Rodman at the Oklawaha River headwaters are also two small Marion County parks which have ramps. They are located just off Highway 316 east of Eureka at the river bridge. These remote ramps are better suited for small boats and 4-wheel drive vehicles.

Lodging in the area is scarce. You may have to travel into Citra, Ocala or Palatka to find a motel. Camping facilities can be found at the Lake Oklawaha Recreation area near the Rodman dam and at Kenwood Landing on the northwest side of the lake.

The Recreation Area is located off Highway 19 just south of the bridge over the barge canal, about 14 miles south of Palatka. Primitive camping is allowed at most of the Corps' public launch ramps around the lake.

Numerous flooded trees and stumps are just under the water's surface while other project upward for 50 feet or more. The famous "stump flats" lie just north of the Barge Canal cut as it stretches through the lake from Kenwood Recreation Area to its outlet on the east side of Rodman. The floating logs make navigation on Rodman hazardous. As a result, great care must be taken when boating out of the marked Cross Florida Barge Canal and Oklawaha River channel. Use extreme caution when moving across the flats and follow the Army Corps of Engineers aids to navigation when possible.

Boaters passing through the Buckman Locks can access the impoundment from the St. Johns River. Rental boats and motors are available at the many fishing camps on the big river around Welaka. The locks are generally open between 8:00 a.m. and 4:30 p.m., but it is wise to check their current schedule.

Like most waters that are difficult to navigate and fish, a guide is usually worthwhile. For information on Rodman or to secure a professional guide, contact Dan Thurmond at his Professional Guide Service, P.O. Box 313, Orange Springs, FL 32182; phone (904)867-1565. He has several guides, in addition to himself, that work out of his guide service.

2

WITHLACOOCHEE WONDERS

THE SHINER WAS nervous. It tugged on my tackle and darted one way, then another. The water's surface bulged with the movement of a big predator and the baitfish took to the air. It smacked down beside a pad and was quickly engulfed.

I let the line feed off my level-wind spool for a couple of seconds and set back hard on the seven-foot rod. The big fish then exploded on the surface and bulldozed through the lilies. Heavy pressure stopped her run, and Dan headed our boat in that direction. Pads submerged and twisted as the line remained taut and the bass plowed ahead.

Trophy bass are numerous in Lakes Rousseau and Tsala Apopka and the pits, canals and channels of the Withlacoochee River.

Slowly I worked the fish through the entanglements, and as she approached the boat, the big bass made her one and only jump. The line was still around one pad stem when my partner netted the largemouth. The eight pounder was slightly larger than the one I had caught just 30 minutes earlier. Like the other encounter, we took several photos and then returned the bass to the water. The shiner's tail stuck out of her throat as she swam off, none the worse for wear.

The cool temperatures made our winter clothing appropriate for this adventure on the Withlacoochee River. The bass were cooperating, as they often do on the waterway. Cold weather is no time to miss the action on the river, according to my frequent fishing partner, guide Dan Thurmond. Another largemouth that pushed seven pounds was soon being photographed and further proved Dan's point.

Despite the excellent cool weather big bass action, the Withlacoochee River, the Backwaters and Lake Rousseau near Dunnellon, and Lake Tsala Apopka just off the river's west bank, are some of the most overlooked largemouth bass waters in the state. About the only time these waters don't produce is when they are at flood stage. The rest of the year, they produce numerous bass and some real giants. The largest bass are normally taken during the first three months of the year, but a shiner angler may locate a trophy just about any time.

This Withlacoochee River is actually one of two in Florida. It is the furthest south of the two and actually originates in the Green Swamp Area in northern Polk County. It is one of four rivers born in that swamp (the other three are the Hillsborough, Peace and Oklawaha), but it is the largest by water volume and longest of the four waterways. For a dozen miles or so, until it reaches Pasco County, it is indistinguishable from the swamp.

The 100-plus-mile long river flows into the Withlacoochee State Forest, along the Citrus County boundary. In all, the river passes through, or forms the boundary of, seven counties. It is one of the few rivers in the U.S. which flows north (there are two others in Florida). Once it reaches the town of Dunnellon, it turns 90 degrees and heads west toward Yankeetown at the Gulf. To further clear up any confusion, note that the northern Withlacochee, which flows south, originates in Southern Georgia and joins the Suwannee River near Live Oak.

RIVER HISTORY

Withlacoochee was named by the Seminole Indians and means, "Little Great Water." Over 150 years ago, at a crossing near Dunnellon, a historic battle ensued between Chief Osceola's Seminoles and U.S. Army troops under General Duncan Clinch. The river remains largely unchanged today. The town, about 21 miles west of Interstate 75 and the most prominent along the river, was founded in the late 19th century about the time the state discovered phosphate reserves and a mining demand for such.

Today, the mining and timber industries that once flourished are gone. Marks of the early days remain, though. Old phosphate pits dot the edges of the Withlacoochee River south from Dunnellon. Many of the pits have the old pilings left in them, just below the surface of the water. A boater has to be extremely careful when moving about in them, but that's where the bass are usually located.

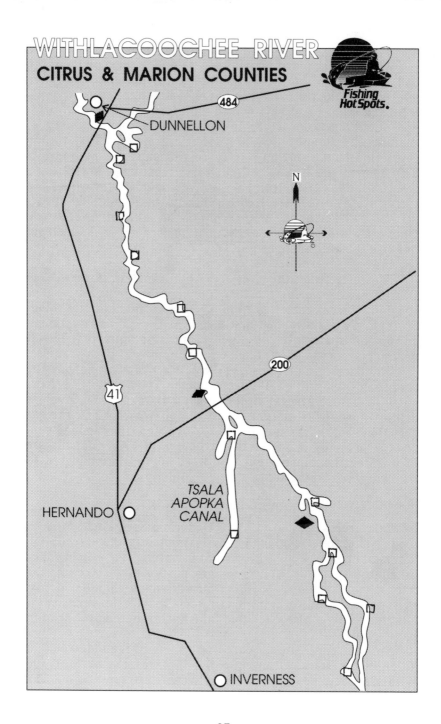

WITHLACOOCHEE RIVER
CITRUS & MARION COUNTIES

Fishing Hot Spots.

484

DUNNELLON

N

200

41

TSALA
APOPKA
CANAL

HERNANDO

INVERNESS

We had launched at the Highway 41 bridge ramp on the south end of Dunnellon, and it wasn't long before Thurmond and I were motoring off the river into one of the numerous old pits. Cypress trees and fallen brush surrounded the 15-acre pothole. Lily pads and other vegetation clung to some portions of the perimeter shallows. The tannic waters stained by organic acids from rotting vegetation in the surrounding cypress swamps and pine forests help to make the area one of the "bassiest-looking" in the state.

Thurmond opts to troll huge native shiners during winter and spring. He'll normally troll with an electric motor until his clients get action. Then, he will drop anchor on the newly-discovered fish. Once in a while, when he locates some "banked up" cover, he'll put out the anchor and tight-line shiners into and underneath the vegetation.

The guide fishes the river area approximately 25 times each season, usually during the first four months of the year. It is roughly 35 miles each way from his base of operations at Silver Springs. Once on the Withlacoochee at Dunnellon, Thurmond and his guide party will typically cover some nine miles of waterway upstream from the public launch ramp.

Downstream, he'll run along the well-marked channel into the sprawling, stump-filled Backwaters area. The depth varies from about 15 to over 60 feet along the inundated river channel. Average depth around the reservoir is about 10 feet. Weather-beaten signs sometimes help newcomers find their way around the impoundment and to fish camps, etc. Some of the older private signs not only aid in marking the channel but also were appropriately placed to indicate good fishing areas.

IMPOUNDMENT OPTION

Lake Rousseau and the Withlacoochee Backwaters form an old, 14-mile long impoundment constructed in the early 1900s. When built, the 4,000-acre reservoir covered an existing lake called Rousseau, so the lower six-mile portion of the lake kept the same name. The upper portion which extends eight miles almost to Dunnellon is known as the Backwaters. Both sections encompass hundreds of acres of flooded trees which were not removed prior to impounding.

No clear-cutting took place on this one of the oldest lunker holes in the state. Consequently, the area fed by both the Withlacoochee and Rainbow Rivers is a jungle of bass habitat. The

The beautiful Tsala Apopka lakes offer generally overlooked bassin'.

infestation of underwater stumps and tree stems are an ever-present danger to boaters, but they also attract bass. While the snags, log jams and dead falls limit access to some areas, they also make for a fisherman's delight. Expansive weed beds, water hyacinths and other types lie along the flats and they provide bass action in the cooler months.

Thurmond has fished Lake Rousseau downstream of Dunnellon and found the action very good trolling along the dam near Inglis in the winter months. Although the dam was originally built for power generation, the hydroelectric plant has been long abandoned. Today, powerful largemouth frequent the area. There is plenty of shoreline cover, but Thurmond prefers the offshore structure in the form of submerged hydrilla. During the cool weather, vegetation growth is at a minimum.

Smart anglers will also check out the water hyacinth beds and lily pads that are profuse throughout the system. Most are in three to seven foot of water near other cover and deep water, and that's where the big bass can be found. Shiners are what many anglers use to draw them from the often dense habitat. Productive spots with names like Big Timber, Bird Island, Pig Pen Area, Old Mill, Horseshoe Lake and Alligator Pass shouldn't be passed up.

GIANT LARGEMOUTH HAPPENINGS

The guide's largest fish from the river, caught in the spring a few years ago, weighed 13-3/4 pounds. Thurmond and a client were trolling a large shiner; the bass came up to hit it, but it wouldn't take it. They trolled over the fish three additional passes, and each time the bass would knock the nine-inch shiner out of the water. It never did grab the baitfish, however.

"I told my client that if that fish came up one more time, we were going to anchor down and put out a smaller shiner," recalls Thurmond. "She did on the next pass and we dropped our anchors. I opened up the bait well and got a peanut shiner - it wasn't over three inches long - and hooked it on."

That bait didn't last but five seconds, according to the bearded guide. The trophy fish was soon landed. The slab shiner found the big bass, but for some reason, the largemouth wouldn't take the bait.

"I think that in the spring, when the bass are heavy with roe, they won't eat the big shiners," Thurmond reasons. "They have so much pressure in them already, that don't want to add a big shiner to their bellies and increase that pressure. You can locate them with the large shiners, but you'll catch them better with the smaller baitfish."

"A large shiner will not get real nervous around a two or three pound bass," he points out, "but when a fish that's big enough to eat him swims by, that big shiner will try to climb the wall."

A friend caught four bass over nine pounds on one day from the Withlacoochee, but Dan's best day on the river was the day they caught the 13-3/4 pounder - they also landed an 8-1/2 pounder from the phosphate pits. The guide has had numerous catches similar to ours that one day, and, in fact, on another day on the river with him, I caught two bass that weighed between six and eight pounds. We had launched at the county boat ramp off County Road 39 that day and covered entirely different waters. A canal and several tributaries and false channels were our focus on that outing.

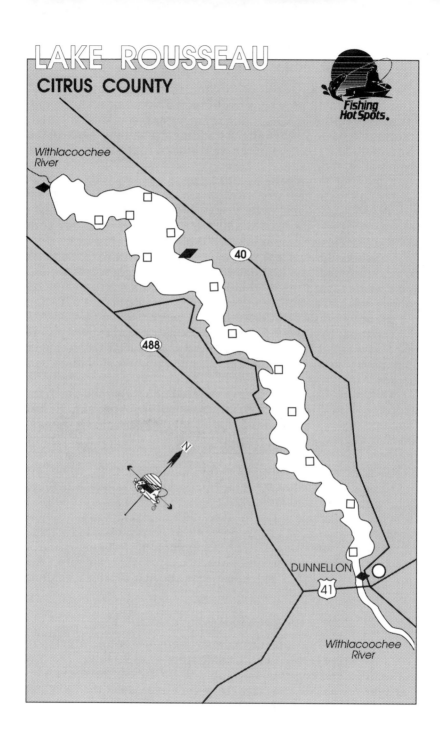

Records Sometimes Get Away

"I feel that this is one of two bodies of water in the state of Florida that could produce a world record bass," says Thurmond. "The other is Rodman, but this body of water is very similar to that reservoir. You don't have all the standing timber in this area of the river, including Lake Rousseau, that you do in Rodman. There is timber here, though."

"This area produces a lot of 14 and 15 pound bass, and that is what makes me believe that a world record possibility exists here," says the bearded guide. "We lost a giant bass here that I'll never forget. Charlie Haag, from Miami, was fishing with me and we both saw the fish clearly before it broke the hook right in two."

"The fish didn't break the line or the pole, it broke the hook right at the bend," he explains. "The fish hit an eight inch shiner, and Charlie turned the fish once. It came by the boat and kept on going with a steady pull. The rod slapped the side of the boat when the 5/0 hook broke. He reeled it in an we both cried."

"Without having the fish in your hand, it's hard to say how big that bass was, but Charlie has caught another with me that was over 14 pounds. We both agreed that this one was three pounds bigger anyway."

Thurmond usually fishes two trolled bobber rigs and one tight line as he works his boat via electric motor along the banks. He has found that the waters near the banks are brushy and that is big bass habitat. Occasionally, he'll drop anchors and still-fish a pocket or specific structure.

Largemouth never seemed to lose their appetite for a live bait or artificial. Thurmond uses plugs and worms occasionally in these waters, and notes that largemouth over 15 pounds have been taken from the Withlacoochee on the fare. Worms and jerkbaits account for quite a few trophy bass, as do weedless spoons and spinnerbaits. At times, top water plugs fool a big largemouth, and crankbaits can be especially effective in cooler weather. Fronts seem to affect the spring-fed river waters much less than they do Florida's shallow natural lakes.

Environmental Details

Some of the pits off the main river are deep while others are very shallow. Average depths range from 15 to 30 foot. The pits were mined and continuously pumped dry during the operation. Once the phosphate was removed, a cut was made at the river and the pits were allowed to flood.

The Withlacoochee River is considered by most observers to be among the cleanest and best-preserved in the state. The pristine waters meander through cypress swamps, pine forests and marshes and deer, otter and a virtual aviary of rare birds are often noticed along the banks of the softly-flowing river. Osprey glide overhead, and blue herons, wood storks and gallinules scan the shallows. Animal and bird watchers can certainly enjoy a day on this river.

Turtles sun themselves on stumps and dead-falls along the banks, and alligators sink quietly beneath the surface as a boat approaches close by. An occasional, forest-surrounded shack left from early logging days may appear near the shoreline. Long stretches of the Withlacoochee, although privately owned, are mostly protected by remoteness and inaccessibility. Additionally, the Southwest Florida Water Management District owns more than 40 miles of river. Other portions of the waterway are protected by conservation and recreation agencies.

The typical flat glassy surface of the river mirrors the green hammocks of cypress, oak, cedar and ash. Spanish moss drapes the forest and palmettos line the shore in some areas. Springs bubble up in the swamps along the banks of the Withlacoochee. About the only disturbance along most of the shores these days are from archaeologists that may dig through a mound at the river's edge, searching for Indian artifacts.

The U.S. Park Service manages Lake Rousseau for fishing and other recreation. South of the river, a barge canal connects the lake with the Gulf of Mexico, but commercial users have mostly abandoned the canal, according to the U.S. Army Corps of Engineers' lock tender. While municipal sewage pollution from several towns along the waterway was once a minor problem, dumping has stopped, and the 2,000 square mile drainage basin quickly allowed the river to recover. Fortunately, the bass fishing never suffered.

Tsala Apopka Lakes Summer Bass

Bass action heats up in the summer on the Citrus County chain of lakes called Tsala Apopka. The beautiful waters, with the Indian name meaning "many lakes," lie 50 miles north of Tampa. The chain consists of three primary "pools" with control structures between each one. They include over 23,000 acres of water that stretch from Floral City to the town of Hernando. The chain is realistically a series of about 50 interconnected, cypress-lined lakes, ponds and marshes.

The Floral City pool is the largest at around 9,800 acres and consist of Floral City, Tussock and Hampton Lakes, among other smaller finger lakes. The deeper Inverness pool contains about 8,000 acres and includes lakes Davis, Big Spivey, Little Spivey, Big Henderson and Little Henderson. Moccasin Slough and the man-made Cove and East Lakes can be accessed by canals. The marshy Hernando pool, consisting of 6,200 acres, contains lakes Bellamy, Croft, Hernando, Point Lonesome, Todd and VanNess and others.

Tsala Apopka is bounded on the east by the Withlacoochee, on the west by U.S. Highway 41, the south by S.R. 48 and the north by S.R. 200. The lake record is reportedly over 15 pounds, and numerous bass in the 6 to 10 pound category are taken each year. The waters average from 12 to 16 feet in depth and have many holes over 20 feet deep. These waters are some of the most beautiful in the state that I've fished and most productive!

Each body of picturesque water has its own unique features; some are surrounded by marsh and prairie; others abut high, rolling hammocks. Cypress trees and huge oaks draped with Spanish moss surround others. Islands are numerous, and the shoreline is the most irregular of any in the entire state. Tannin-stained creeks, canals and boat trails go behind and though many areas.

Lake Davis, south of S.R. 44, may be the best summer water, according to Cypress Lodge owner, Bud Andrews. The guide, who fishes the entire chain, says the most effective rig for bass action is the "do-nothing" that employs a thin, pencil-type worm. He suggests a Culprit Pen Worm with its "rake" tail pinched off. Hook it through the belly (wacky-style) with a 4/0 hook and add a 12-inch long leader and No. 10 swivel to complete the productive rig. The worm action closely imitates a nightcrawler that would be twisting and wiggling when washed into a lake.

Use spinning tackle with eight-pound test line and cast the rig to the pads and grass on Davis. Allow it 10 seconds or so to sink to the sandy bottom, and then use a twitching motion to slowly retrieve the bait. You'll get plenty of action there and on Big and Little Henderson Lake to the north of Lake Davis. Andrews and two fellow guides and their clients caught over 2,400 bass from the chain during one ten-week period.

Lake And River Details

For overnight accommodations, check out the towns surrounding the area, such as Dunnellon and Inverness, well in

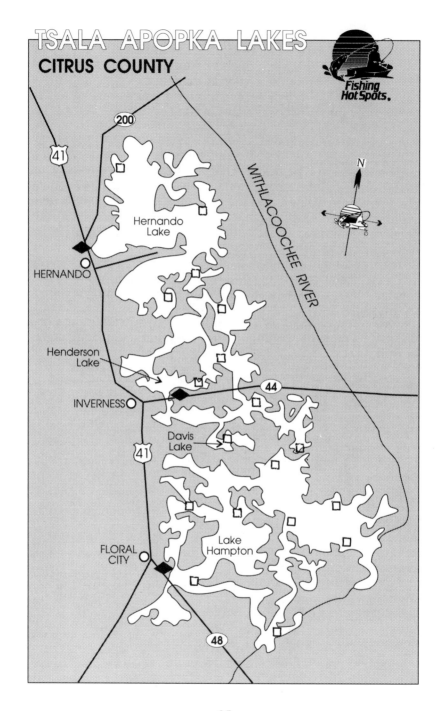

TSALA APOPKA LAKES
CITRUS COUNTY

Fishing Hot Spots.

200

41

Hernando Lake

HERNANDO

WITHLACOOCHEE RIVER

N

Henderson Lake

INVERNESS

44

Davis Lake

41

FLORAL CITY

Lake Hampton

48

advance of any cold-weather trip. They are limited during the "season" when snow birds flock to the state, so it's best to have reservations. Several motels have their own docks and rental boats. A few fish camps border the lakes and river, and several public ramps are scattered about as well. The later are well marked on the major road ways. Campgrounds in the area are numerous and scenic for those traveling with an RV or tent.

The Withlacoochee River and its lakes offer many miles of meandering bass trails through sand hills harboring dense hardwood swamps. Due to the number of false channels in the lower end of the river and in Tsala Apopka, a good topo map or guide is wise to avoid confusion. Local guides are not plentiful, but a few exist. Some can be booked direct while others are available through the fish camps or resorts.

For one of those pleasant fishing experiences in pristine waters and a chance at the trophy bass of a lifetime, consider Florida's southern Withlacoochee watershed. Anytime is the right time to try your luck here!

For further information, contact the Florida Game and Fresh Water Fish Commission, Central Region, 1239 SW 10th St., Ocala, Florida 32674 or phone (904) 629-8162.

3

BASS CAPITAL OF THE RIVER

BETWEEN THE TOWNS of Georgetown and Palatka, the largest river in the state offers one of the most productive and popular largemouth bass fisheries in the country. Called the "Bass Capital of the World," this section of the north-flowing St. Johns river has fertile waters and multitudes of big largemouth. The river in this section meanders slowly through extensive floodplains and is influenced by waters from Crescent Lake via Dunns Creek and from the Oklawaha River system, a major tributary, and by tides.

The St. Johns River between Palatka and Lake George has a long-time reputation as being the bass capital of the world!

The river here is one that is relatively easily patterned. When the current slows as the river passes through lakes, like George and Monroe further downstream, fish scatter. In the river itself, however, current plays an important role in the life of shad and bass. An interesting type of schooling situation develops here, revolving around the existence of current.

"The bass like to locate in an area where the current actually speeds up, usually due to a more narrow section of the river or an underwater structure that causes an upwelling turmoil in the current," points out taxidermist Ken Daubert. "They like to position themselves out of the force of the current and wait until the shad are pulled overhead by the moving water. These areas are consistent producers of schooling activity, but they are more unpredictable as to when they will produce."

The currents here are influenced by factors other than gradient. The sluggish flow of the St. Johns River from Lake George to the town of Palatka is affected by daily tidal movements to and from the Atlantic Ocean. Downstream flow exists about three-fourths of the time, but high tides and strong northeasterly winds can reverse the flow over this section of the river. Heavy winds can also accelerate the outgoing tide.

I'll normally fish the submerged structures in the river, keeping my bait in contact with them if at all possible. I prefer a slow-moving outgoing tide for maximum action and try to avoid fast currents by fishing the edges of structures then. Some places will produce bass on an incoming tide, while others will yield largemouth on an outgoing tide.

The tide controls the forage; when it is going out, it pulls the bait out of the grassbeds, out of the creeks and sloughs, and when running in, it pushes the forage up into those areas. Bass may feed on either tide movement, but when the tide moves, so do the largemouth to adjust. A "dead" tide may be tough, so the key to catching bass when this happens is to try to find some moving water.

Surface plugs, buzzbaits and subsurface vibration emitters are a good choice in the stained river waters. Currents give increased life to curly tailed worms, even at slower retrieve rates. They also make timing of the cast and retrieve important, as well as accuracy. Those unfamiliar with the effects of a river may need time to adjust.

There is usually enough water to cover throughout this section of the river to make mistakes in casting and still catch bass. With Dunns Creek and Crescent Lake, the waters to cover are many. The latter might even give one a respite from the currents of the river and creek.

CRESCENT LAKE ACTION

Crescent Lake is one of my personal favorites. It has yielded some impressive catches for me over the past 20 years and hasn't really waned. It is normally an excellent bass fishery year around. The eelgrass beds, pilings and lily pads are especially productive in the cooler months. One of my best catches of bass came by wading the shore on a cold November day.

Some good areas to wade are the reed beds on Shell Hill Point in the spring and fall. Plastic worms and surface plugs with a tail-spinner are productive. The reed, pad and grass combination surrounding Bear Island yields bass all year to wade fishermen.

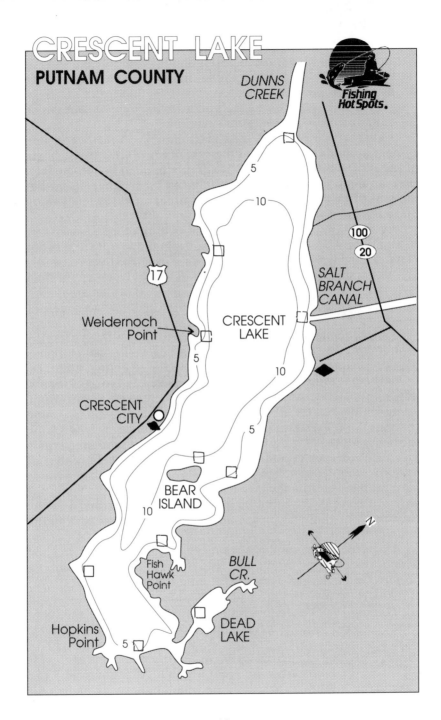

CRESCENT LAKE

PUTNAM COUNTY

DUNNS CREEK

Fishing Hot Spots.

100
20

SALT BRANCH CANAL

CRESCENT LAKE

Weidernoch Point

5

10

CRESCENT CITY

BEAR ISLAND

10

Fish Hawk Point

BULL CR.

Hopkins Point

5

DEAD LAKE

5

17

N

The areas in two to four feet of water on the north side are good in the fall, while similar areas on the south side of the island yield big spring bass. Waders fish weedless spoons, spinnerbaits and large plastic worms and make long casts in the shallow cover. They work the baits very slowly for maximum action.

Another way to catch this lake's bass is to fish an in-line spinner around the eelgrass at the base of the cypress trees. Some of the lake shallows offer a fairly sharp dropoff at about five feet. In some areas, the bottom quickly falls to 12 feet. That means that the bass often move into the shallows to feed and then may move off to deeper waters on a drop.

Orlando angler Steve Hamman and I were on the lake early one summer day when the bass started knocking shad out from under piers. I quickly switched from a plastic worm to a silver finish Big "N" and took three bass on three casts. The bass followed the shad into the heavy grass beds which ran up to the pier area. We followed. We methodically worked the area and within a couple of hours had 32 pounds of largemouth in our livewell.

During the late summer and fall, you can often find schooling bass action like that on Crescent Lake. Schooling bass will push panicky shad to the surface most likely in the mornings, evenings, or just before afternoon thunderstorms. Keep an eye out for gulls hovering or diving. Any bird activity is certainly worth investigating.

Some of the best ares to find schooling bass action is around the mouth of Crescent Lake during the week when boat traffic through the area is at a minimum. Another good schooling area is just off Weidernoch Point's abundant grass. Don't believe that all bass are schooler size, however. Two largemouth over 17 pounds have been taken from the lake within the last ten years. While not part of Crescent, it should be noted that tiny Lake Stella in the Crescent City limits has given up two bass over 16 pounds in the same period.

Numerous docks and pilings on Crescent Lake provide good bass action. The pilings off Hopkins Point are particularly productive for largemouth in the spring months. Guides favor crankbaits or plastic worms and fish them tight to the wooden structures. They'll also toss Rat-L-Traps to the pilings and try to bump "wood" without getting hung on anything other than a largemouth.

The lily pads in Grimsley Cove and those in the southeast corner of the lake harbor fish year around. The mouth of Dead Lake in the southeast corner is deep, and the shoreline on its west

Flippin' the outer bends in Dunns Creek is often and effective technique for summer bass.

bank offers submerged brush and laydown timber. The most effective bait in this area is a Texas-rigged plastic worm. Fish it in depths of 5 to 10 feet for best results.

DUNNS CREEK

There are several good areas along Dunns Creek that offer good fishing. The mouth of Dunns Creek has a number of fallen trees on shore. When they fell, the root system tore loose and a depression was left at the shore. Such places inundated with water make good hiding spots for bass. Numerous pads along the creek are prime spots for flippin' a plastic worm. Bass move from the deeper waters into the emergent vegetation to feed early and late in the day.

Dunns Creek crosses Murphy Creek on the south side of Rat Island, and bass congregate along the dropoffs from three feet down to the 20 along the channel. The creek is blessed with canals that offer excellent fishing for both spawning and pre-spawn bass.

For best pre-spawn action, use a sonar and locate the sandbars in front of the canals.

The canals nearest any creek bend are especially good for bass in the summer on an outgoing tide. The mouths of canals entering any of these flowing waters are always productive spots for the baits. Use lightweight lures and let the current wash it along for maximum success. Also flip a Texas-rigged plastic worm into the pads commonly found in the canals.

Largemouth hold in the outer bends of Dunns Creek during the summer and winter months. The sharpest bends yield bass in the late winter and summer months. Those with brushy banks and sharp drops are most productive. Outside bends with submerged trees and dense grass cover in four to five feet of water are also prime areas in the creek to fish. Check out the bars, points and dropoffs found by sonar with a deep-running crankbait or bottom-bumping plastic bait, like a Carolina-rigged worm.

WHERE TO LOOK IN THE RIVER

The docks, pilings and bulkheads along the St. Johns on either side have produced some monster bass. They provide excellent cover, forage and protection. Forage and shade are abundant in these areas, and the water temperature can be slightly cooler and richer in oxygen.

Piers and pilings along the river come in all shapes, sizes, lengths and conditions. Some on the river even have small cabins on the end several hundred feet from shore. The most important characteristic in a good dock is close proximity to deep water, usually something over five feet. If it doesn't have deep water, then your chances of finding bass under it are minimized.

You'll also want to find river docks with the most shade, the wider ones which cast a larger shadow. The more protection a dock or row of pilings offer, the better the fishing. The density and size of the support posts beneath the dock is always an important consideration. The more dense (number of posts, cross-members near the water, etc.) the more productive a pier can be. The larger in diameter that these posts are, the better they usually prove to be also.

One of the better areas along the river is Wilson Cove, which offers excellent submerged structure in the form of sunken barges, old pilings and laydown trees in two to eight feet of water. Harts Point is a very sharp bend in the river with extensive eelgrass

42

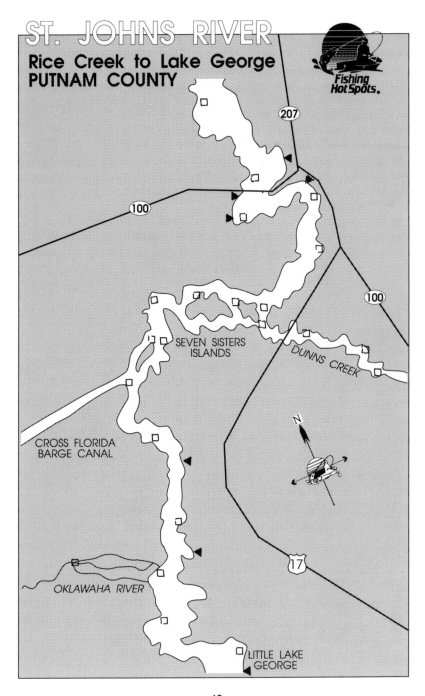

ST. JOHNS RIVER
Rice Creek to Lake George
PUTNAM COUNTY

Fishing Hot Spots.

207

100

100

SEVEN SISTERS
ISLANDS

DUNNS CREEK

N

CROSS FLORIDA
BARGE CANAL

17

OKLAWAHA RIVER

LITTLE LAKE
GEORGE

43

patches, wooden docks and bass. Porters Cove is a good bass area that has shallow grass cover lying off the edge of the main river channel. It yields big spring bass, as does the perimeter of Buzzard Island.

Other good spots along the river are the grasslines at the end of Polly Island and along Horseshoe Point. Check out the grassy humps in the middle of the river always for concentrations of bass. The weedline along the mouth of Murphy Creek and the pilings also produce bass. So do the lily pad beds and other vegetation in waters three to seven feet deep around the Seven Sisters Islands. Concentrate on the points, hyacinth banks and numerous laydown trees near the overgrown shoreline.

One of my favorite spots is the railroad trestle at Buffalo Bluff. I've taken huge largemouth off both shorelines on either side of the bridge. You'll find a variety of cover there including vegetation, submerged driftwood and fallen timber. When the tide is going out, fish the outside of the river bend, and on an incoming tide, fish the shallow bar and grassy dropoff. In the winter, work the fallen timber cover in the five to six feet of water along the south shoreline just east of the bridge.

Another of my favorite spots is Stokes Island. I'll fish the south end on an outgoing tide, and on an incoming tide, move to the northern point of the island. Also, I'll fish the submerged tree-littered shore along the east bank, and nearby, the grassbeds at the mouth of Trout Creek. Schooling bass often move into these areas from the river. When not in the shallower water, schoolers are found around the deeper channels where tributaries enter or leave the river, and at wide spots in the river.

The first quarter mile of the Cross Florida Barge Canal can provide bass action when water is being released from the locks. Fish the dropoff down to 16 feet and around the mouth of the canal. Grass flats that extend from the shoreline almost to the edge of the channel all along the river provide good year-round bass action. Also, don't overlook lily pads around the numerous islands and back in the coves off the main channel.

Turkey Island at the mouth of Welaka Springs has numerous laydown trees in water depth ranging down to 20 feet. Areas of coontail moss and eelgrass in combination are prime spots to catch fish. The popular lily pad line extending from the relatively clear Oklawaha River to the north is also productive.

In Little Lake George, a few spots stand out. On the east side off Beecher Point is a deep water grassline that extends south into

The brush in the river attracts big bass in the dead of winter.

Mud Creek Cove. Also work the boat docks in the summer and the flats in the spring during spawning times. Croaker Hole Cove offers islands of hydrilla that attract bass in the spring, summer and fall. The spring hole and the numerous docks in the back of Fruitland Cove both yield big largemouth.

SUNSHINE/STRIPER OPTIONS

The stripers in the St. Johns River system are riverine populations rather than the nomadic variety that migrate from saltwater to freshwater to breed. The fish do move around in search of warmer water in the winter and cooler water in the summer. Striper hot spots in this section of the river during the summer include the cool waters of the Oklawaha River. Late

...trations of stripers occur around the
...the river.

...en year-round in this section of the
...monly caught during cooler weather
...l. The feeder-creek mouths and deep
...centrations of stripers and hybrid
...oth fish species typically travel in
...time in open water, so trolling the
...to locate them. Anglers normally employ
...ng or spinning tackle with lines testing 20 to 30

Rat-L-Traps, in-line spinners, shad-resembling crankbaits and 1/2 to 1-ounce white or yellow jigs are best bets to fool one of the battlers. The most effective artificials for striped bass are those whose size is selected based on the size of forage on which the stripers are feeding and on the depth being fished.

Fishing the cool-water tributaries in the summer and winter is also smart if after a trophy striper. Fishing live bait in deep flowing waters is an excellent pattern during the hotter months. Live threadfin shad, three to five-inches long, are the deadliest summer bait for trophy-size stripers when found in concentrations. Small bluegill and shiners and saltwater shrimp are other good live baits to fish. Fishing with live bait at night with a bright light as a fish attractor is another. The fish are more active after dark.

Supplemental striped bass stocking began in 1970 and hybrid striped bass have been stocked since 1981. In the past three years over one million each striped bass and sunshine bass fry have been stocked in this section of the river. Additionally, stocking figures show introduction of almost 3/4 of a million sunshine fingerlings during the same period.

Few stripers exceed 25 pounds in this section of the St. Johns due to their shorter growing season and increased physical stress resulting from elevated water temperatures. In fact, without cool water refuges and the present stocking rates employed, a severe reduction in their lifespan and total population in this section of the St. Johns would be inevitable.

RIVER AND LAKE DETAILS

This section of the St. Johns River is about 60 miles long and has a maximum depth of around 30 feet. The average depth is closer to 20 feet. The 15,960-acre Crescent Lake has a maximum depth of 14 feet and averages about 10 feet. Its waters discharge into Dunns Creek which empties into the St. Johns.

The Oklawaha River is a major tributary discharging into this section of the river near the town of Welaka. The 125 mile long Oklawaha is the largest tributary in the entire St. Johns drainage. The St. Johns River is connected to Rodman Reservoir by the six-mile long Cross Florida Barge Canal.

Eelgrass, coontail and southern naiad are the submerged vegetation varieties found along many of the shallow bars and shoreline areas in the river and in Crescent Lake. Spatterdock or yellow pond lily, and alligator weed are emergent plant communities that grow along the river in waters of four to six feet. All of the above are important vegetation for forage and bass.

There are numerous public launch ramps along this section of the river. On the west side of the river is Palatka's popular J.G. Goodwin Riverfront Park which has two double-wide concrete ramps, and on the east side of the river off highway 207 in East Palatka is a Putnam County Boat Ramp. About 2 miles south of Palatka on the west side of the river is Putnam County's Lundy Road ramp.

Further south, off highway 309 on the east side of the river is the very popular Shell Harbor Ramp, and about 3 miles south of that one in the town of Welaka are the Highway 308B/Elm Street boat ramps. On Crescent Lake, only one public ramp exists, that being off highway 17 in Crescent City. The double-wide ramp is on the west side of the lake at the end of Central Avenue.

Several good guides work this section of the river. A couple are Terry LaCoss/Amelia Angler, phone (904) 261-2870, and Peter Thliveros, North Florida Bass Guides, 1306 S. Edgewood Ave., Jacksonville, FL 32205; phone (904) 772-7927.

4

LAKE GEORGE MONSTER BASS

SCHOOLING BASS PUSHED panicky shad to the surface about 200 yards from Daubert's racing johnboat. About 100 yards from the surface action, he shut off his small outboard motor and his 14-foot, double-wide johnboat coasted forward. He lowered his trolling motor and continued his approach toward the bass.

To capitalize on the schooling bass action, the guide knew that he had to get to them quietly and quickly. With the aid of his powerful bow-mounted 34-pound thrust electric, Daubert's aluminum boat neared the breaking fish. He took his foot off the trolling motor switch, and from his stable casting platform selected the appropriate arsenal. Daubert had several rods rigged with various types of tapered flylines; he began his false cast with a standard weight-forward taper.

The second largest lake in the state is one of the most productive trophy bass waters in the country.

Daubert laid the fly softly and accurately in the activity, and set back on the rod almost instantly. A two-pound Lake George largemouth cartwheeled above the threadfin shad scattering about and was quickly brought to the boat for release. Daubert made another long distance cast, twitched the fly a few times with no takers. The feeding activity continued a few yards away with about 12 bass popping shad on the surface at any one time. The expert fly caster made a single back cast and second presentation to the strike zone.

A three-pounder took up Daubert's offer and kept a good bend in the rod until lipped at boatside. The guide quickly released that fish and continued his multiple presentations to what he terms, "a blitz zone." The bass stayed on top in their foraging mood for almost 15 minutes, and Daubert caught and released eight largemouth before the school sounded.

Such action is not uncommon on the lake, and you don't have to fly fish to catch bass from a blitz zone. You do have to keep the lure or fly in the area of the most heated competition, where even the most selective bass is vulnerable. Even after the activity wanes, long distance casts to selective stragglers can be productive.

There are often hundreds of bass attacking shad as far as you can see, and they are loosely organized in groups of six to 12 bass attacking at random. Although they do not generally stay up long, they reveal their location to the observant angler. Fortunately, the bass will readily strike presentations, even when they are not actually chasing shad.

The schooling bass on Lake George are an experience that Daubert, a fishing guide and taxidermist based in Silver Springs, doesn't overlook. In fact, he has frequently experienced the schooling activity common in July and August. He and a client have caught and released 30 to 40 schooling largemouth in one day. Lake George's schooling bass can also be encountered later in the year, but they may be less predictable then.

In the summer, Daubert looks specifically for schooling bass and usually finds them. Although big bass are sometimes caught out of the schools, the main excitement comes from the sheer numbers of smaller largemouth. The aggressiveness with which schoolers attack their prey keeps the guide going back for more.

LOCATING THE SCHOOLERS

The best way to locate school bass is simply to search for them until you find some. Keep moving, and check out the open areas when school bass are most likely to be breaking water, and therefore, be easier to see. Mornings, evenings, just before afternoon thunderstorms and sometimes during overcast weather are prime times to find schoolers. At other times, bass schools will feed in heavy early morning fog. That's when you may have to rely on "sound fishing."

"One morning the fog was so thick that I couldn't see much further than my trolling motor," Daubert told me. "Finding schoolers seemed hopeless, and I thought the fog may last all morning. When I shut the outboard down, all was quiet, except for the sound of breaking fish."

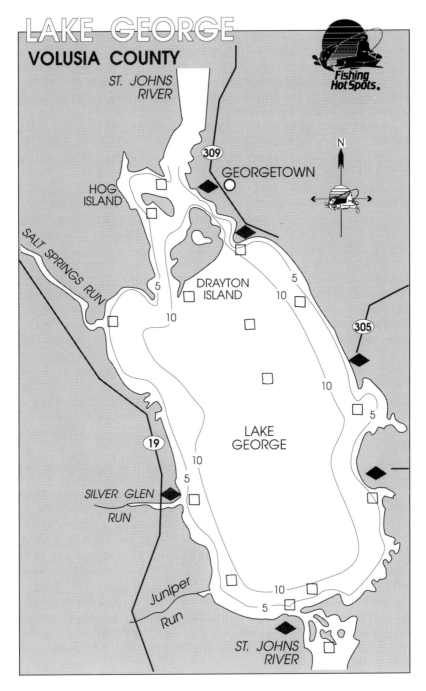

LAKE GEORGE

VOLUSIA COUNTY

ST. JOHNS RIVER

Fishing Hot Spots.

309

GEORGETOWN

N

HOG ISLAND

SALT SPRINGS RUN

5

DRAYTON ISLAND

5

10

10

305

10

5

19

10

LAKE GEORGE

5

SILVER GLEN

RUN

Juniper

Run

10

5

ST. JOHNS RIVER

"It was difficult to determine the direction of the fish, and to complicate matters, there were many schools of bass," says Daubert. "Distances were difficult to guess, so I simply ran the trolling motor until I got close enough to figure out the direction to cast. That was a strange but enjoyable experience. I caught and released over 30 bass before breakfast!"

Thanks to a hard bottom, shallow water and widely scattered activity, wading is very effective here. Lake George is huge, though, and you do need a boat to locate active areas. Wading the flats with boat in tow is a popular way to fish the lake. Most breaking fish are fairly easy to spot; even in early morning sunlight, schooling activity can often be seen as distant sparkling explosions. Keep an eye out for terns or gulls hovering or diving. Any bird activity on George is certainly worth investigating, and just one or two birds may indicate a bass feeding frenzy.

Another indication of impending or submerged feeding action is "nervous water," usually denoted by a break in regular wave patterns. This often indicates schools of shad or bass just beneath the surface. The bass often school in knee deep, off-color water, thick with eel grass. The tips of the eel grass are often protruding through the surface, critically limiting the types of lures that can be effectively utilized.

"Conventional lures such as crankbaits and jigs are out of the question," says Daubert. "Even surface lures with treble hooks can be difficult at times as bass chase the shad right into the shallowest areas and ambush them from the concealment of the eel grass."

The bass average two to three pounds, and are very strong and aggressive, making hard runs and jumping often in the shallow water. The won't easily spook from boats or clumsy waders, but they can sometimes be very suspicious of your offerings.

"The right choice at the end of your line can produce some very busy bass bugging for hours at a time," says Daubert. "Especially if you can catch the edge of a late afternoon thunderstorm which tends to bring on the schooling activity earlier and extends it right through the evening until dark. Lake George is dangerous in a thunderstorm," he cautions. "So search near a safe landing area if thunderstorms are approaching.

Once located, the feeding bass will usually strike a properly presented lure. Bass may make one sporadic blitz, or they may bust the surface for hours. If you are very lucky, you may be able to consistently catch schooling bass for days, weeks, or even months in the same general area!

Docks around the mouth of Lake George and Drayton Island are often good bass habitat.

BIGGER BASS TARGETS

On my first trip to these waters back in 1969, I took two bass that each weighed ten pounds, plus two others that totaled 13 pounds or so. Honestly, the many trips since have not been that productive in terms of lunkers, but the waters here still produce.

Huge expanses of eel grass flats are where the bass often forage. Pilings in Lake George and along the St. Johns on either side have also produced some monster bass for me. Bulkheads, docks, and fallen trees in the Georgetown and Welaka areas hold giant largemouth year around.

Numerous giant largemouth between 12 and 14 pounds are taken from the lake each year. Every few years, a 15 or 16 pounder is caught. February through April are the most popular for trophy bass chasers, when the biggest bass in the lake move shallow to spawn.

The lunker bass fishing in Lake George is influenced by the spawning migration and flows of the tributaries, several large and numerous small springs, and by daily tidal effects. In fact, high tides and strong northeasterly winds can cause reverse flow (north to south) through the lake. Strong currents around the mouth of the river on each end pushes baitfish against submerged structures. Fish these structures keeping the bait in close contact with them on a slow-moving tide. Avoid fast currents by fishing the edges of structures then.

The circular clusters of pilings in the middle of the lake serve as aids for the military bombing range. Fishing is allowed around these bomb targets; live munitions are seldom dropped, but planes wanting to use the targets let anglers know. When an A-6 attack bomber wings by 100 feet from the boat, it is time to move on toward the shoreline.

Based on recent creel surveys by the Florida Game and Fresh Water Fish Commission, Lake George is the top-rated bass fishing water in the state. In an average Florida lake, it takes about four hours to catch a keeping-size bass, according to the Commission. That's a fishing success rate of .25 largemouth per hour. In a good bass lake in the state, anglers haul in a keeper every three hours, which is a .33 fish per hour rate. Research by the Commission biologists has shown that Lake George supports catch rates of .59 in the summer and .40 in the spring.

Tactics, Lures & Bait

The flats on Lake George's perimeter extend from 200 yards to 1,000 yards out into the lake. Select the ones with the densest eel grass beds and those in the deepest water - usually about four feet. Drifting live bait or tossing an artificial from the boat can be productive. From mid-May through September, mid-day fishing in the flats is often a waste of time. Early morning and late afternoon fishing on the flats are still productive, as are fishing the deeper water pilings and docks or a trip to the cool spring waters.

Bass activity shifts from the shallow vegetated areas during hot weather. Higher pH levels in the thin waters cause an adjustment to slightly deeper waters, to more shaded waters, and to those in current. Schools of largemouth may move offshore in the deeper waters of the lake. Schoolers can be found on the north end of the lake around Drayton and Hog Islands, around the deeper channels where the St. Johns enters and leaves the lake and, sometimes, right out in the middle off the dredged navigation channel that traverses the length of the lake.

Schools of largemouth will stuff themselves on shad in open water and then move into the man-made timber on Lake George to relax. Others stay in and around the numerous piers, docks and pilings on a full-time basis. They feed and rest in the comforts of their shady hideaway. The pilings and docks provide excellent

The cove areas on Lake George offer productive spring fishing for largemouth.

cover and protection from predators. Baitfish and crayfish are usually in the vicinity of the rotting wood posts. Shade is abundant in these areas, and the water temperature can be slightly cooler.

Lake George largemouth are usually found shallower than you would normally expect them to be in most lakes, if they're using the piers and docks. Such structures come in all shapes, sizes, lengths and conditions. Many are partially dilapidated and most are wooden. There are about a dozen stands of old pilings in the lake left over from the old days when heavy goods were transported by steamer.

WHERE TO LOOK

The good fishing areas on George are many. The Drayton Island docks and pilings and the boat trails to them, and the sharp dropoffs from nearby weedlines in the area are productive. Find those waters with hard sand bottom and relatively deep water near shore for maximum action. The pilings on and just off Kinsley Point on Drayton Island produces bass year around. Also fish Black Point and its open-water dropoff.

Muddy Cove shallows and the grassline cuts between Hog Island and Saunders Cove offer spring and fall action. The east side of Hog Island and the south side of Rocky Point are feeding flats that often yield bass. The docks and pilings along the Georgetown shoreline and those on the west side of the lake offer bass action in the spring through the fall.

There is often action to be found around the spring runs. Clear Salt Springs Run enters the lake on the west side of Salt Cove, and the mouth of the creek attracts pre-spawn bass. The dropoff at the mouth of Silver Glen Springs Run has a six-foot breakline that attracts largemouth bass. The grass beds around the mouth of Juniper Springs Run also attracts pre-spawn bass. Lunkers often hang out in the open water just off the spring runs' mouth.

The wood pilings at the navigation channel jetty near the mouth of the lake provides excellent fishing throughout the year. Fish on the three-foot side of the jetty during the spring and fall and on the nine-foot side during the heat of summer and cold of winter, when boat traffic is minimal. The best set of shoreline pilings in my mind exist off Nine Mile Point. They have produced hundreds of bass for me over the years. The hard sand bottom makes this a great spot.

Any point on the lake that is swept by current attracts largemouth bass. Irregular weedlines found in Jones and Willow Coves also attract concentrations of largemouth. Willow Point is a feeding flat for spring and fall bass. Savvy fishermen cast the grassline and inside the grass, especially around the row of pilings. Also, concentrate on the holes inside the vegetation and a six-foot breakline offshore.

Big Striper Options

The southernmost range of striped bass in the world resides in Lake George and the St. Johns River system. Striped bass are commonly known for their propensity to cover substantial distances during seasonal migrations. The stripers in Lake George, however, are riverine populations rather than the nomadic saltwater variety that migrate from saltwater to freshwater to breed.

Thermal refuges just off the lake's west shore are used by both stripers and striped bass hybrids during the summer and winter months. The hybrids are, however, less attracted to thermal refuges where water temperatures range from 72 to 75 degrees F. Cool water is present in Silver Glen Springs, Salt Springs and Juniper Springs. Such runs are prime spots for trophy striper.

Striped bass can be taken year-round, but they are most commonly caught in the fall, winter and spring during cooler weather. Late winter and spring concentrations of stripers occur at the jetties, pilings and bombing range in Lake George. The fish typically travel in schools and spend much of their time away from the vegetated shoreline. The offshore pilings are haunts of both stripers and largemouth in George.

Most successful anglers work a shad-colored, deep-running crankbait so that it ricochets off the wooded structure. Others fish live shiners in the daylight or after dark, jigs and plastic grubs, jigging spoons or tail-spinner lures along the bottom. White or chrome Rat-L-Traps are another choice to fool a striped bass around the pilings off the river channel in the lake. Trolling the Bombing Range on the northeast side of the lake is another way to locate striper schools.

Striped bass seldom exceed 20 pounds here, and that's due to increased physical stress resulting from elevated water temperatures. Without cool water refuges and the present stocking rates employed, a severe reduction in their lifespan and population total would be inevitable.

LAKE DETAILS

The 5 mile wide by 13 mile long lake is 46,000 acres and 78 square miles. It averages about 8 feet in depth, but a dredged navigation channel 13 feet deep traverses the lake. There are four sources of inflow around the lake, including the St. Johns River, and the major cool-water spring runs of Juniper, Silver Glen and Salt Springs. Other major springs above the lake are Blue Springs, Alexander Springs and the Wekiva River.

Lake George has about 50 miles of shoreline with a border of profuse vegetation. This extensive littoral zone, primarily of eelgrass, is highly productive fisheries habitat. Other major aquatic plants established in the lake include water hyacinth, coontail, spatterdock (yellow water lily), hydrilla and bulrushes. It's the medium-dense stands of mixed eelgrass and fragrant water lily which typically yield the highest bass catches on Lake George.

This lake between the towns of Georgetown and Astor has a few launch ramps. On the north end off highway 309 is a rough, concrete ramp beside the Drayton Island Ferry Loading Dock. On the southeast side of the lake off Highway 3 about two miles north of Pierson is the Nine Mile Point ramp, and on the southwest side off Highway 40 west of Astor Park is the Jetty Ramp. Most visitors launch on the river in and around either Astor or Georgetown. For guide service contact; Ken Daubert, Rt. 3, Box 587, Silver Springs, FL 32688, or phone (904) 625-3562.

ST. JOHNS
BEST OF THE BEST

IN 30 YEARS OF fishing the St. Johns River, Bob Stonewater has figured out the flowage. My good friend knows what the current does, where it hits, where the drop offs are formed, and how structure may be piled up on the bottom. Knowing how to "read" this section of the mighty St. Johns is what helped the guide amass hundreds of king-size bass.

The affable 40-year old DeLand professional and his clients have caught nine bass over 13 pounds from the river. In his guide duties, Stonewater fishes up to 50 miles either side of the highway 192 bridge.

Between Lake Monroe and the southern end of Lake George lies perhaps the state's best largemouth fishing!

He prefers to fish deep creeks that are flowing into, or leaving, the main river channel. A quick drop off on each side of the point, down to 12 feet of water, is ideal. The deep water right up to the bank allows a trophy bass to trap the forage against it. Weed patch cover extending out from the shoreline, and eel grass nearby on the inner bend of the river in four feet of water, make for perfect habitat, according to Stonewater.

"It's not the size of the creek, but the depth of water and amount of current that's important," reveals the guide. "If it's fairly deep, and has some cover, that's sufficient."

King-size bass look for such spots to lay out of the St. Johns current and feed. A cut bank or quick drop at the shore makes such habitat ideal, Stonewater points out. A lunker can chase a forage fish right up underneath the surface-bound weeds and the prey nnot get away. Rains increase water flow in the river and tributaries, so a smart angler will look for those natural feeding holes with current. A lot of new bait is washed into the river, and it hugs the shoreline tightly as it is washed downstream.

Trophy-size river bass, snug in their habitat, are lazy. They realize that it's hard to strike and connect with forage fish in open water. The prey often escapes the pursuit of a lunker in deep channels. There is little to limit the movement of a fleeing baitfish, and big bass generally know that.

St. Johns' monster largemouth will move a little to feed, but not far. They prefer a feeding area with some current that will wash forage to them. An ideal feeding area would be a two-foot-deep sand bank that drops to ten feet and then gets shallow again. Bass can lie in the deeper trough and move onto feeding grounds to pin the prey against the bank.

While fishing large native shiners, Stonewater has developed some concepts that are productive when applied to plugs. Big forage fish give off slow vibrations when moving through current. Big crankbaits, like Bagley's Killer "B 3," have a slow wiggle too, producing similar sound waves that attract big bass. In fact, in one recent month using crankbaits, the guide and clients caught seven bass from the St. Johns that ranged from seven to 10-3/4 pounds. During the same period, their shiners accounted for 27 largemouth which scaled from six to 11-1/4 pounds.

Summer and fall are better for numbers of feeding fish on this portion of the St. Johns. There's always some bass feeding in the river and its creeks. Some river areas, though, get a lot of pressure, so conservation is paramount. The guide prefers to fish for lunker bass during the non-spawning seasons for several reasons. The big bass are more concentrated in deeper water, and they are pursued less by the hordes of anglers that are out after a spawner in the spring.

Bass not on shallow banks are not early feeders. Of all Stonewater's bass over ten pounds caught during the past year (numbering somewhere around 100) for example, only two were caught before 8 a.m. His log reveals that the majority in each month were taken between 10 a.m. and 3 p.m.

River Characteristics & Influences

The St. Johns in Lake and Volusia Counties meanders slowly through extensive floodplains, including large, shallow lakes such

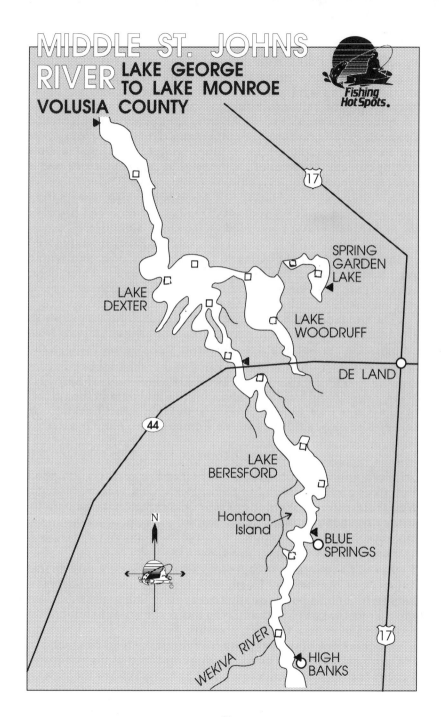

MIDDLE ST. JOHNS
RIVER
LAKE GEORGE TO LAKE MONROE
VOLUSIA COUNTY

Fishing Hot Spots.

17

SPRING GARDEN LAKE

LAKE DEXTER

LAKE WOODRUFF

DE LAND

44

LAKE BERESFORD

N

Hontoon Island

BLUE SPRINGS

WEKIVA RIVER

17

HIGH BANKS

as Dexter and Beresford. Several creeks and waterways flow sluggishly through lowland swamps and wetlands before entering the river. Such places offer the largemouth angler numerous spots to cast a lure or bait successfully.

Between Lakes Monroe and Dexter are numerous small canals, and many have a good dropoff at their mouth. The river area there can be characterized by wide, long, straight runs, and a slow moving current. Largemouth congregate at canal entrances, and it is not uncommon to quickly catch several from such an area. In the river section between Dexter and Monroe are also many spring runs which can make for some exciting bass action. The fish love the stable temperature provided by the clear tributaries.

Water levels in this section of the St. Johns River are influenced by the daily tide of the Atlantic Ocean. High tides and strong northeasterly winds can even cause reverse flow. Tides here, however, are not as much a factor on the fishing productivity as they are further north on the river.

The productivity here is among the state's best, according to creel surveys by the Florida Game and Fresh Water Fish Commission. In fact, the river area from Lake Dexter through the Crows Bluff portion was recently listed as the very best bass fishery in Florida. The top bass area produced two bass every three hours in the summer and almost two bass every four hours in the spring. In an average Florida lake, it takes about four hours to catch one keeper-size bass, according to the Commission.

TACTICS, LURES & BAIT

Vegetation such as cattails, bulrushes and eelgrass, are good bass areas on the river and in Lakes Dexter and Woodruff. Lake Woodruff offers bass action year around, but is especially productive in the spring. Lake Beresford can be productive during cooler weather along its bonnet-covered shoreline and underneath its docks when the summer sun is around.

In the Lake Dexter area, bass prefer river banks with sparse eelgrass and brush tops. North of Astor, logs and brush lying in deep water or on a point usually attract bass. Use a sonar unit and move along the river bends until you locate the prime habitat. This is the area of heaviest fishing pressure.

If fishing one of the numerous canals off the river channel, use Texas-rigged worms and deep-running crankbaits along the drops. Anchor the boat upstream of a canal and toss toward the mouth,

The bass in this section of the St. Johns are often fat and healthy, like this one caught north of Astor.

bumping the fare along the bottom. The canal mouths in the river offer a productive refuge when white caps are on the lakes.

Most canals have a uniform depth, and that depth is seldom the same as that of the lake or river it enters. Thus, a five to 10-foot drop is usually found at the point where the canal digging ended. Usually, this is good bass habitat for tossing light lures. The same tactics can be used where canals cross each other; one may have been dug deeper in order to obtain a good start on fill for the dikes.

There are numerous sandbar points at the confluence of tributaries which flow in and out of the main river channel. Morrison and Blue Creeks are two good bass areas north of Astor. During the spring, brush in these places can yield big bass.

In late summer and early fall, schooling bass are abundant in this stretch of the river when American shad fingerlings dimple the water's surface as they move downriver to the ocean. Small crankbaits, spoons and jigs will fool the schoolers.

WHERE TO LOOK

There are a number of great spots to check out for concentrations of bass in this section of the river. The point across from Blue Island offers scattered vegetation and submerged brush in 5 to 8 feet of water. Trophy-size bass hang out here and on nearby Morrison Island Point. The east bank of the river just south of the Highway 40 bridge in Astor offers a sharp drop and a few wooden pilings which attract bass.

Eelgrass patches on the bottom all along the river channel make excellent feeding areas for largemouth. Both the channel side and false channel side of Lungren Island and the deep water pilings near Bluffton Point are productive spots for largemouth. The weedbeds in two to seven feet of water off Dexter Island at the mouth of the lake also yield largemouth all year long.

Clear spring water from Alexander Springs Run enters the river between Lakes Dexter and Woodruff, and largemouth often hold near the mouth. The lily pads just off the numerous islands in the area offer a chance at giant bass. The water is only two to four feet deep but the largemouth move along them in the spring. The mouth of Lake Woodruff is another good spot to try. It is best on week days when boat traffic through the area is at a minimum.

The mouths of Norris Dead River and St. Francis Dead River both offer abundant lily pad fields and bass action. Numerous submerged brush piles are found all along the section of the river shoreline between Dexter and Monroe. There is also a good dropoff down to about 10 feet of water along most of the river bank. The lily pads at the south end of Lake Beresford harbor bass, as do the floating weedbeds throughout this section.

The mouth of Blue Springs south of Orange City and the shallow vegetation and brushy shoreline near the mouth of the Wekiva River offers bass action. Use sonar and a good map to locate the main channel dropoff in front of these two tributaries. Also check out any mussel beds you may come across; they attract the entire food chain, including large concentrations of bass.

STRIPED BASS OPTION

The significant striped bass fishery on the St. Johns depends on hatchery stockings. One million sunshine bass and over two million striped bass have been stocked in this portion of the river during the past three years. Both can be taken from this section of the river year-round, but they are most commonly caught from January through April during cool and windy weather.

Both stripers and hybrid striped bass cover substantial distances during seasonal migrations in this section of the St. Johns River.

The bass fishing in the Dexter area of the river is rated to be the best in the state.

Behind some of this movement is the striper's need for cool water in the summer. The spring waters that exist along this section of the St. Johns represent thermal refuges, and as a result these areas attract stripers and hybrid stripers. In the winter and early spring, concentrations of stripers migrate to the power plant outflow on the west end of Lake Monroe where waters are typically warmer than the river.

Fishing the cooler spring runs in the summer and winter is smart if after a big striper. Fishing live bait in flowing waters is an excellent pattern during the hotter months. Live threadfin shad, three to five inches long, are the deadliest summer bait for large stripers when found in concentrations. Small bluegill and shiners are other good live baits to fish. Fishing with live bait at night with a bright light as a fish attractor is another. The fish are more active after dark.

The pilings of major bridges are where concentrations of stripers and hybrid stripers also appear. Rat-L-Traps, in-line spinners, shad-resembling crankbaits and 1/2- to 1-ounce white or yellow jigs are best bets to fool a striped bass around the pilings in a river channel or on one of the lakes. Sunshine bass (hybrids) and stripers typically weigh two to four pounds and travel in schools. Once the fish move deep, jigging spoons are a good choice.

River and Lake Details

The St. Johns River is over 307 miles long with a drainage area of approximately one-sixth of the entire state. This portion of the river is about 40 miles long and is from 10 to 20 feet deep along most stretches. It also includes three lakes. Lake Beresford is 800 acres and has a maximum depth of seven feet. Lake Woodruff covers 2,200 acres and is five feet deep, while Lake Dexter is 1,902 acres and has a maximum depth of 16 feet. The average depth of all three lakes is only four to five feet.

Numerous springs are located in the river or discharge into it. Major springs are Blue Springs above Lake Beresford, DeLeon Springs off Spring Garden Lake and Alexander Springs (fourth largest in the state) located just above Lake Dexter. The Wekiva River, entering the St. Johns below Lake Monroe, is the only major cool water tributary discharging into this section of the St. Johns.

Moderately abundant vegetation exists in the river with the heaviest growths found in shallow sloughs, false river channels and the shallow lakes. Major aquatic vegetation in the river includes water hyacinth, eelgrass, spatterdock and some bulrushes. Yellow pond lily grows in water depths of four to eight feet, and is abundant on Lake Woodruff, and water hyacinths are the prevalent type on Lake Dexter. Drastic changes in types of vegetation can occur each year due to water level fluctuations, weather, and aquatic plant control.

Numerous county and commercial ramps scattered along this section of the river make access easy. Many are free to the public. At Astor, for example, there are two just south of the highway 40 bridge within a few blocks of each other. Both are on the west side of the river off Front Street. One is the Pearl Street ramp, and the other is the Clair/Butler Street ramp.

Further south off highway 17 on the east side of Spring Garden Lake off Lake Woodruff is the De Leon Springs State Park. The beautiful park charges an entrance fee and is about three miles by water to Lake Woodruff. A more accessible ramp (to the river), the Ed Stone Park, is located on the northeast side of the Highway 44 bridge on the river. Two other ramps on the river are located off Highway 17-92. One is west of Orange City on French Avenue, and the second is in DeBary on Highbanks Road.

Those wanting to contact the guide for bookings or information on the St. Johns River can write Bob Stonewater, Trophy Bass Guide Service, 179 Glenwood Rd., DeLand, FL 32720; phone (904) 736-7120.

6

SANFORD MUSSELS

CATTAILS, BULRUSHES and other types of vegetation are profuse on Lake Monroe, but the bass are not always pulled directly from such cover. Instead, they may be near the cover in slightly deeper water. What attracts the normally habitat-intense largemouth to open water areas just outside of the vegetation may surprise some.

It's very difficult to find a mussel bed situation. My initial exposure to the phenomena occurred several years back on my first trip to the lake. I was fishing with Charlie Foster, a professional angler from North Carolina, and we were both tossing Texas-rigged worms in three feet of water along the bulrush beds on the north shore. The first 100 yards were unproductive, but we did notice some movement, apparently by bass, in the stalks.

Discoveries in Sanford area lakes and the St. Johns River can lead to great bassin'.

Charlie had his trolling motor on high speed as we quickly covered the area until fish were found. We each missed a strike, so we slowed down the boat. Fishing relatively fast leaves a few "unfished" spots to the person in the rear of the boat - me. It was to one of those places that I cast a crankbait.

I had only retrieved it about three feet when a fat two-pounder pounced on it. Charlie's long second cast to the same area hooked a bass of about 1-1/2 pounds. He then turned the boat to anchor on that productive spot. We fished it hard primarily with worms and crankbaits for the following hour and caught 15 more largemouth from an area about 10 feet wide and 20 feet long.

Our strikes were always several feet away from the cover, and we wondered after the first three fish why the school of bass were in that spot. My crankbait finally came up with a snail on it - a mussel. Four casts later, another mussel, and we had our answer. I had heard of largemouth congregating over mussel beds, but this was the first time that I had experienced it.

The mussel bed was a gold mine of bass. With little for a bass to get entangled, we were able to land every fish hooked. Finally, the action slowed, and Charlie pulled anchors and headed away. I tossed a huge worm into the spot, my "last cast."

It had just reached the bottom when my arms were almost jerked out of their sockets. I set back hard on the big fish and after a good fight and three exciting jumps Charlie netted the seven pounder. That, the biggest in the pocket of mussels, had neglected our constant bombardment of smaller fare for over an hour. It couldn't resist the 12-inch worm that I lobbed there, however.

Charlie again turned the boat and re-anchored on that snail bed, but we only caught one more bass in the following 45 minutes. We left with a memorable experience of the mussel beds of Lake Monroe. A bottom-bumping crankbait had paid big dividends that day by discovering our school of bass.

Unfortunately, the mussel beds tend to relocate after a while. Once you find them, however, you may be able to catch bass off them for several weeks. Obviously, the better ones are those a little ways off the vegetation that most anglers cast toward. They can be occasionally found all over the lake; a major bass tournament was won off one located in the southwest corner of Monroe.

OTHER BASS STRUCTURES

When you can't find a "golden" snail bed, the vegetation does hold good bassin'. Largemouth relate to any type of structure on the Lake Monroe and just above it on the river, whether it's weeds, shells or wood pilings.

On another trip to the Lake Monroe, my partner and I worked our worm fare around the points and pockets in the rushes. We took about 20 bass by concentrating in areas where we had one strike. We would then go back and forth in that area for several minutes looking for additional fish. Where we found one, usually two or three others would be nearby. We circled one tiny island of vegetation three times to amass five largemouth. It was only ten

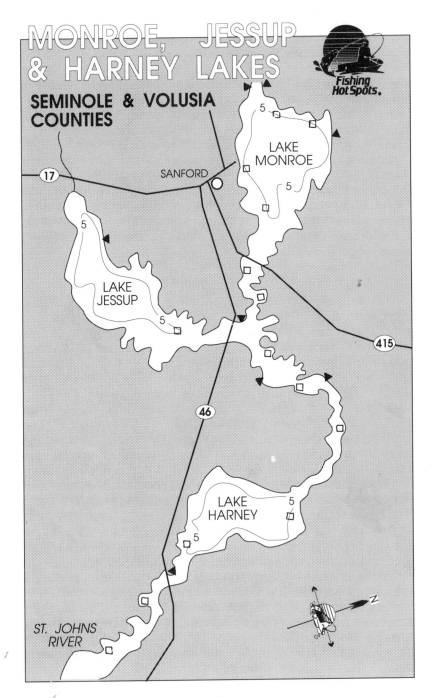

MONROE, JESSUP & HARNEY LAKES

SEMINOLE & VOLUSIA COUNTIES

Fishing Hot Spots.

LAKE MONROE

SANFORD

17

LAKE JESSUP

415

46

LAKE HARNEY

ST. JOHNS RIVER

feet wide by 30 in length, but our persistence paid off. My seven-inch worm fooled the largest, a five pounder.

We moved to some pilings on the south side of the lake and tossed vibrating plugs to catch three more bass, and then had a two-pound crappie slam the plug. There are several sets of pilings on the Sanford-side of the lake, and often they hold a variety of fish. Pilings on the north side of the lake can also be productive. Crankbaits take their share around the wood structure.

Lake Monroe has a well deserved big bass reputation. Some of the best fishing for trophies is along man-made bulkheads. Shiners, large worms, crankbaits and spinnerbaits can be effective on the giants. Fish near the wood structure and use heavy line and tackle to hoist out a big bass, if you should be so lucky. If the monsters of the lake aren't feeding, there are places nearby to catch numbers of bass ... for the action.

Upstream Possibilities

The St. Johns River current upstream from Monroe is usually substantial. That allows drifting anglers to use the trolling motor primarily for directional correction. Others may want to anchor and work a specific cut in the bank or a deep bend. In the river channel one thing is for certain: an un-anchored boat is not a still one. In the 20-mile stretch of river between Lakes Monroe and Harney, the boat will drift downstream at three to five mph.

Fighting such a current with the electric motor is not wise, even for those sporting the super powerful 24-volt models. The batteries will soon be drained if you persist in moving upstream for great distances sans the outboard. The current is at its maximum during the rainy season when the upper St. Johns is relatively high.

Bass in the section of the river between Monroe and Lake Harney then are suckers for baitfish or minnow-imitating lures. During the spring, when the American shad makes a spawning run up from the Atlantic, bass are moving in the currents, focusing on minnow prey. The shad's offspring hang out in the swifter river runs, and through the early summer, largemouth aren't far away.

In the summer and early fall heat, forage fish are more scarce, and bass move around in shallower waters searching for a variety of food fare. Artificials, particularly plastic worms, account for numerous fish then. Waters are often low in the late summer during periods of little rainfall, and the fishing is relegated to the river channels. Few of the sloughs and marsh cuts off the main channel have adequate water depth for bass.

The St. Johns River just above the lake is highly productive in normal water conditions.

Sandy sloughs with some form of fresh water supply may remain productive, but many dry up or lose water to a point where their heavily-silted bottoms are near the surface. Navigating the low water in that portion of the river is not too difficult. Further upstream, the maze of false channels, shallow sloughs and wide spots in the St. Johns can be deceiving and problematic during low water levels. Regardless, if you are exploring any portion of the river above Lake Monroe for the first time, proceed carefully.

OUTSIDE RIVER BENDS

My brother, Ron, wanted to experience some big bass fishing during a visit from Kansas. I called friend Bob Stonewater and arranged to meet him at the public ramp in Sanford the following morning. Bob guides on the lake and river on either side and is more knowledgeable about the area than anyone I know.

We took off from the marina at about 8 a.m. and planed across the lake and into the river. We motored upstream just two bends before Bob shut off the big Evinrude. Eight to 10-inch shiners swam circles in the live well awaiting their calling. We quickly placed three out in the current and began a drift toward the lake.

The lively baitfish were working the points and pockets in the vegetation perfectly. The lead shiner got blown out of the water as

71

it moved through the first bend. The bass missed. A following baitfish wasn't so lucky, and the seven pound bass also got more than it bargained for - a 5/0 hook. I quickly landed that fish and released it.

The boat continued to drift along with our bobber-supported shiners working nearby until Ron got some action. A six pound largemouth was his prize, and then the three of took turns catching bass. We made about four passes through that 3/4 of a mile stretch and caught bass every time. They ranged from about four pounds up to that very first seven pounder.

The outside bends in the river often drop to 20 feet or more, and we had quite a bit of action in such places. The river in that area, though, has a very irregular shoreline, so the points and pockets in the shoreline vegetation also contained bass. In fact, we caught bass right at the river's mouth at Lake Monroe.

I've fished above the lake with Stonewater often, and we usually do well. On every trip that I can recall to the area we have taken five to 15 bass, and the largest usually pushes eight to 10 pounds. The DeLand guide definitely knows what the Sanford bass are looking for. He'll fish the baitfish on one trip and toss artificials on another.

THE OVERLOOKED TOMOKA

One of the most beautiful little bass streams is the Tomoka River in northern Volusia County. It's not long, but the waterway is lined with cabbage palm trees, making fishing around a sunset or sunrise a memorable experience. From its beginnings in the Tomoka Wildlife Management Area, the river winds it way northeast. The brackish river empties into the salty Halifax River near Ormond Beach, so there are not many miles of freshwater to fish. What is there, however, holds bass.

Upstream of the highway 40 bridge is a narrow stream that poses navigational problems for large boats. Along the banks, however, are fallen trees and partially submerged logs. Also present are numerous largemouth. This section of the river is the least pressured and probably most productive. For the close-up casting, spinning tackle is normally used, and some of the big bass caught are four or five pounds.

Between the highway 40 bridge and the U.S. 1 bridge is a stretch of open river accessible to any size of bass boat. Plenty of bank-side targets here yield bass. Small creeks and canals enter

Most of Monroe's largemouth are moving about in the cattails on the lake's perimeter.

this section of the river which is both salinity and tidal influenced. Bass anglers will toss topwater plugs, plastic worms and jerkbaits around the shallow structure and crankbaits and vibrating plugs around the bars and dropoffs in the channel.

Rains and rising waters seem to turn on the Tomoka bass. Some guides on the river have caught and released over 100 in a day's time. Such days are perfect. Not all fish in the freshwater part of the stream are yearlings; some of the bass have exceeded 10 pounds.

It's not unusual here to catch a bass from one side of a log and a snook or redfish from the other. The fishery below U.S. 1 is primarily saltwater. There are plenty of good launching ramps on the river, including the Tomoka State Park and the U.S. 1 bridge, so access is easy.

LAKE DETAILS

Lake Monroe at Sanford is 9,406 acres and averages five feet in depth. It has a maximum depth of 18 feet. Two fish attractors of citrus tree limbs concentrate fish in Lake Monroe. They cover an area of approximately 100 feet by 100 feet and are at least four feet under the surface. The locations are in open water and are marked by floating buoys painted white, black and orange. One lies in seven feet of water near the mouth of the river just south of the Enterprise power plant and opposite a public boat ramp. The other lies in eight feet of water on the northwest side of the lake at the confluence of three ship channels.

There are three public ramps on Lake Monroe: West of Sanford off Highway 17-92 just north of the draw bridge is Lake Monroe Park and a fee ramp. Off Highway 17/92 just south of the draw bridge is the popular Lake Monroe Wayside Park, and on the north side of the lake at Enterprise is the Lakeshore Drive ramp.

7

PASTURE/BORDER BASS

STAINED WATERS PUSHED at our anchored boat. Shiners tugged at the corks as the flowage further infiltrated the St. Johns marsh plain. The baitfish had come to life quickly and drifted into the vegetation bordering the small ditch off the main river channel. The outlet, no wider than 15 feet or so, had a significant current moving through it. The eight-foot depth, sharp sloping shoreline and aquatic vegetation on the banks made this spot ideal.

Largemouth fishing along the upper St. Johns River is a sight.

The first shiner placed along the bank "jumped up" through the weeds and fell on top of them, out of the water. The bait will do that once in a while to get away from a big bass, but the bass will also tear apart the weeds to get at its prey.

By then, my shiner had drifted to the same overgrown spot on the shoreline. The bobber bounced twice and submerged. I stood and began slowly taking in the slack.

Predictably, this bass moved like most other river bass, toward the center of the small flowage. After a bass takes the bait, it will normally move somewhere. My largemouth swam straight out to the middle and then turned around and headed back under the cover where she had taken the bait. That's also a fairly typical move for big fish, and I was ready.

I tightened the line keeping the rod tip up at a 45 degree angle from the horizon and set the hook. The 10-pounder rolled to the surface and headed toward the shoreline entanglements. Slowly, I pressured her back to Bob's waiting net. We snapped a few photos, carefully measured her length and girth and watched the trophy swim off.

The current seemed to be moving into the tributary, and I was puzzled. We were in the upper St. Johns River, far from any tidal effects, and there had not been a heavy rain in the headwaters flood plain which might cause such an occurrence. The ditch was actually a fork of the main river between Lakes Jessup and Harney, which only flowed during relatively high waters, according to my partner. The small channel is dry in places downstream during normal water levels. That morning we caught and released four other big bass averaging around five pounds each.

This pasture-bound river section is sometimes a bewildering maze of channels that twists through treeless grasslands that encompass lakes Harney, Jessup and Puzzle. Tannic acid-stained waters flow past Brahma cattle and egrets, the sole shoreline inhabitants. Palmetto hammocks and sawgrass bogs dot the tropical plain.

Hundreds of bass over 10 pounds have been taken from the lonely stretches of river between Lakes Jessup and Puzzle. The fishing pressure along the primitive water course is minimal, although Cocoa, Titusville and Orlando are just a short drive away.

LAKE JESSUP TO HARNEY

Several creeks and waterways, including the tributary lake, Lake Jessup, flow sluggishly through lowland swamps and wetlands before entering this section of the river. Lake Jessup lies just off the St. Johns' channel and covers 10,011 acres. It has a maximum depth of only seven feet and averages just four feet deep.

Lake Jessup received treated effluent until recent years, and still today extensive cattle ranching occurs on much of its floodplain. That's an additional source of nutrients that makes Lake Jessup, typically, have the overall highest pH readings on this section of the river. The vegetation, consisting primarily of giant reed, water fern, paragrass and pennywort, adds to the pH values during high sun times.

Largemouth school off the grassy points in the lake during the summer. Cast to the cover in two to four feet of water and bring bottom huggers down the drop into the channel. The vegetation around Bird Island is sometimes productive for bass during the spring months.

The stretch of narrow, twisting river as it passes Lake Jessup meanders through a grassy plain, sawgrass bogs and vegetated banks well infiltrated with bass. The vegetation growth in the river

The small creeks off the upper St. Johns River can provide some thrilling bass action, even from the bank.

is substantial along the shoreline and offers the heaviest growths in the shallow sloughs, false river channels and shallow potholes off the main channel. The vegetation includes hydrilla, water hyacinth, coontail, eelgrass, water shield, spatterdock and bulrushes.

Crow's Landing, a popular bass fishing spot lies at the outlet of Lake Jessup. Just upstream is Mullet Lake, a shallow body of water that, other than at its mouth, offers little in the way of fishing opportunity and poses a navigation threat during low water periods. The mouth of Mullet Lake slough has a two to nine-foot dropoff that produces schooling largemouth bass in the spring and early summer months.

The river current in this stretch of the river is usually substantial. The boat will drift downstream at three to five mph, so fighting such a current with the electric motor is not wise, even for those sporting the super powerful 24-volt models. The currents do allow drifting anglers to use the trolling motor primarily for directional correction. The current is at its maximum during the rainy season when the St. Johns is relatively high.

The mouth of Mud Lake provides good bass fishing in the spring, summer and fall when water levels are high. Fish the vegetation edges and submerged brush on points in three to five feet of water for action.

The false channels off the main river usually have lily pads in two to four feet of water and good year around bass fishing. Trophy bass are present in these channels around spawning time and in the cuts off the deeper sections of the river during the wet early summer days when water levels are high. Also check out the lily pads and weedbeds around the small backwater areas.

During the spawning months, the mouths of a couple of canals in the area can yield pre-spawn largemouth. Fish along the edge of the grass on both the channel side and the slough during high water times. The deeper river shoreline will have bass holding on submerged brush and logs.

The river twists through the Lemon Bluff area north of highway 46 where sandbars and schooling bass are numerous. Submerged brush and logs in the bends there produce giant largemouth. The river channel in the area does a lot of twisting but it's fairly easy to follow. Deep Creek, Indian Mound Slough, and LeFils Slough are nearby bass waters. The channel of Deep Creek near its confluence with the St. Johns is a good spot to locate largemouth bass. The bass congregate in the brush-filled waters which vary from four to six feet here year around.

FROM LAKE HARNEY TO PUZZLE

Lake Harney covers 6,058 acres and averages about five feet in depth. Predominant vegetation includes about 600 acres each of hydrilla and eelgrass, and less acreage of several other grasses. The lake has the remains of the old sawmill town, Osceola, on its eastern shore. Only pilings remain as evidence of the 1900's town. This lake is not known as a great bass water; most of the bass angling effort around the shallow lake occurs in the river on either side of the lake.

Largemouth bass do school at the mouth of Lake Harney in the two to seven-foot waters. This late spring and summer action is best on week days when boat traffic through the area is at a minimum. Use weedless spoons near the profuse vegetation or Rat-L-Traps in front of the weedy areas when searching for the schoolers. At the mouth of Underhill and Gopher Sloughs, largemouth bass often congregate around the vegetation during spring and early summer showers.

The river eddies off the current produce best between Lake Harney and Puzzle Lake. The latter, so called because of its maze of channels, is the confluence of two main runs. The eddies off the current produce best here. The river's bass fishing can be extremely hot or cold, depending upon the water level. Angling is most productive when fishing the swimming worm rig, an open-hook six inch worm with a kink at the bend.

The grassy islands, river points and pockets on the upstream side of Lake Harney offers some spring and fall bass action. The dead river channels offer good bass fishing in its abundant vegetation during high water times. Fish the water that are 4 feet or more, if possible.

The bank vegetation around the mouth of the Econlockhatchee River yields largemouth in the spring and early summer when the water is flowing from rainfall in the basin. The Econlockhatchee River flows through unspoiled areas of cypress trees and enters the St. Johns River between Lakes Harney and Puzzle and is a source of excessive nutrients from the Orlando metropolitan area and cattle operations in its watershed.

Drainage consists of primarily runoff and rainfall, so the river fluctuates quite a bit, as much as eight feet. Most of the boat traffic in the upper section of the river are canoes that can navigate the narrow, snag-infested waterway easily. Few of the canoers even fish for bass. There are some 35 miles of accessible water, more than anyone could fish in a day.

The shallow bulrush and reed patches in Puzzle Lake hold largemouth in the spring. Check out the three to four foot depths near the abundant vegetation when water is flowing. The mouth of Puzzle Lake, although only two to four feet deep, yields largemouth year around for those that don't get lost trying to find it. The river channel splits in this area where the waters range from three to nine feet deep.

Tactics, Lures & Bait

During a drought, you can forget about fishing much of the river area between the lakes. When the upper river is within its banks during the late summer and early fall, largemouth are more active and concentrated there than elsewhere on the waterway. When out of its banks, as it may be in the late fall, the river can expand to being a mile wide, and that level makes the fishing tough.

Trophy bass often show a preference for large river shiners served in the deep outer bends, while hot weather largemouth frequently "school up" on the numerous sandbars along the 25 to 70 foot wide river. In the spring, the fishing grounds throughout this section are usually narrow, so heavy angling activities and boat traffic can hamper productive trips.

Fishing the sloughs may be the answer to the increased boat activity. A productive slough will be deep with an active flowage from the river channel. A quick drop off, down to eight to 12 feet of water, and deep water right up to the bank is ideal for a trophy bass to trap the forage against. A weed patch cover extending three feet out from the shoreline and eel grass nearby on the inner bend of the river is perfect. It's not the size of the creek, but the depth of water, amount of current and the cover present, that's important.

Most of the bass lie along brushy or highly vegetated banks just after a rain shower. As the water flow increases in the river or tributaries, bass move into the natural feeding holes with current. "Fresh" bait is washed into the river, and it's usually hugging the shoreline tightly as it washes downstream.

Your cast will have to present the lure close to any river monster. They seldom move far to feed, preferring an area with some current that will wash forage to them. You may have to cast prime river structure 30 times and return to the same spot four or five times during the day to catch a lunker. A big fish will eat a mouthful and then might not feed the rest of that day.

Sandy sloughs with some form of fresh water supply may remain productive, but many dry up or lose water to a point where their heavily-silted bottoms are near the surface. The outside bends in the river, however, often drop to 20 feet or more. The river in this area has a very irregular shoreline, so the points and pockets in the shoreline vegetation usually contain bass.

In general, high water allows fish to disperse into all the river and into the floodplain marsh. Low water levels concentrated bass in the deeper river sections and mainstream lakes. In the summer and early fall heat, forage fish are more scarce, and bass move around in shallower waters searching for a variety of food fare. Artificials, particularly plastic worms, account for numerous fish then.

Waters are often low in the late summer during periods of little rainfall, and the fishing is relegated to the deeper river channels only, which is where bass are concentrated. When it's hot, largemouth bass activity shifts from the shallow vegetated areas. Higher pH levels in the thin waters cause an adjustment to slightly deeper waters, to more shaded waters and to those in current. Schools of largemouth may move offshore in the deeper waters of the lake. In fact, schooling bass push panicky shad to the surface frequently in July and August.

Schoolers can be found around the deeper channels where the St. Johns enters and leaves the lakes, where other tributaries and sloughs enter the river and, sometimes, at wide spots in the river. School bass are most likely to be breaking water in the mornings, evenings, just before afternoon thunderstorms and sometimes during overcast weather. Keep an eye out for terns or gulls

Just off S.R. 46 east of Sanford lies some of the best river fishing for bass.

hovering or diving. Any bird activity is certainly worth investigating. Try a vibrating plug or topwater lure when the activity is on top.

RAMP & GUIDE DETAILS

There are several public ramps in the area. On the northwest corner of the Lake Jessup bridge on Highway 46 and Old Geneva Road is the Cameron Wight Park and a double concrete ramp. On Lake Jessup off highways 425 and 427 about three miles south of Sanford is the Lake Jessup Park ramp. About seven miles east of Sanford on the river is Mullet Lake Park. The turn off to it is about two miles past the Lake Jessup bridge on Highway 46.

On the river off highway 415 is the popular Lemon Bluff ramp, and on the south end of Lake Harney off highway 46 is the C.S. Lee Park Launch Area. For guide service on the lakes and river in this area, contact Bob Stonewater's Trophy Bass Guide Service, 179 Glenwood Rd., DeLand, FL 32720; phone (904) 736-7120.

8

THE RENOWN
WEST HARRIS CHAIN

VERY FEW BASSMEN familiar with the fishing opportunities of the Harris Chain of Lakes will go elsewhere. Plenty of largemouth and waters to roam in their search are the attraction. Even giant bass are caught in the chain, particularly those lakes on the western side.

The nine lakes of the Harris, or Oklawaha Chain located primarily in Lake County comprise about 76,000 acres. This chapter covers three: Lakes Griffin, Harris and Little Harris. Lake Griffin and Lake Harris are the second and third largest lakes in the chain, respectively.

The western portion of the Harris Chain offers some of the best largemouth bass fishing in the state.

Lake Harris is the most popular water on the chain. It's a pretty lake; huge rafts of lily pads and shorelines sculptured in palms and cypress trees draped with Spanish moss make this one of the chain's most esthetic lakes. The pad beds hold spawning bass and the small canals with overhanging brush produce all spring and into the summer for anglers who 'flip' worm rigs beneath the tree limbs.

Duck weed in the backs of some canals can produce some big bass for those anglers who "crash" a heavy spoon or rubber "Top Dog" through the vegetation. It will 'part' and allow the lure to reach down to some attentive bass.

Like most of the chain's waters, Lake Harris is relatively shallow. While the deepest water lying just off the southern shoreline is 28 feet, only a few other spots can be found deeper than 14 feet. Some are dredge holes located near the mouth of

Dead River. Locals crawl a Carolina-rigged worm slowly on the bottom around the rocky ledges.

Fishing the rapid drop from the first point northwest of the Highway 19 bridge westward for a couple hundred yards can be productive for lunker bass that move from the depths to feed in the grass.

The grassline lies in three to four feet of water, which is relatively deep for shoreline cover and produces bass year round. Spoons do well in the real heavy grass, over eel grass, and around hyacinths while spinnerbaits account for lots of bass in the more sparse grass patches. Summertime anglers 'flip' these weedbeds with a plastic worm.

Productive maidencane grassbeds and lily pads in three to six feet of water exist around Long Island directly offshore from Lake Park on the east shoreline, Johnson's Point on the north shoreline, and the gradually curving point on the east shore just north of Long Island. All produce heavy stringers of largemouth, as do the areas adjacent to the mouth of Helena Run. The Palatlakaha River (canal) is an excellent clear water spawning area that bass are attracted to February through April.

The cove north of Long Island is a perennial spawning ground for largemouth. In the spring, bass are taken on buzzbaits and spinnerbaits behind the grass and Rat-L-Traps on the outer edge of the cover. Anglers who flip a plastic worm into the edge of the vegetation on the perimeter of the cove also find largemouth action.

The wider Ninth Street canals on the west side of the lake are productive during the spring. Pads grow in 3 to 7 feet of water, and most anglers toss plastic worms, crankbaits, and jerk baits. The water is relatively clear, but the deep water and hydrilla attract bass to the area year around. Knowledgeable anglers will fish their lures very slowly around the submerged vegetation.

IMPRESSIVE CATCH

A crowded live well on this lake is not unusual. On one productive day, a local guide and client caught 27 largemouth, releasing most. The nine largest were most impressive. An 8-1/2 pounder anchored the catch, which also included a 7-1/2 pounder, two bass at six pounds each, three in the five pound range, a four pound largemouth, and a 3-1/2 pound specimen.

Lake Harris is under-fished, and yet is one of the hottest lakes in terms of productivity around Central Florida. The biggest

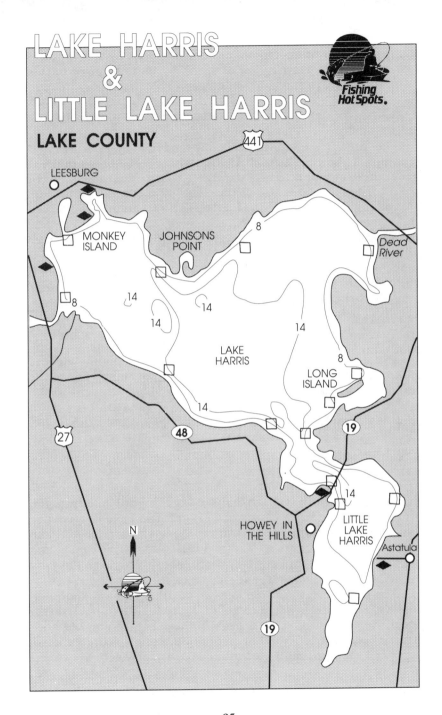

LAKE HARRIS
&
LITTLE LAKE HARRIS

LAKE COUNTY

Fishing
Hot Spots.

441

LEESBURG

MONKEY
ISLAND

JOHNSONS
POINT

8

Dead
River

8

14

14

14

LAKE
HARRIS

14

14

8

LONG
ISLAND

27

48

19

14

N

HOWEY IN
THE HILLS

LITTLE
LAKE
HARRIS

Astatula

19

stringers in the warmer months on the chain come from deep water structure in Lake Harris. Texas-rigged worms in black or purple hues, Rat-L-Traps and Norman's Deep Little N's are favorites of successful anglers. So are plastic tube-type baits, like Gitzits, jerkbaits, like Rapalas, and topwater prop baits, like the Griffin Jerkin' Sam.

One productive location is below the Highway 19 bridge that separates Lake Harris from its little sister. The bass are often under the bridge or nearby in the grass. That general area is one of my favorites on the entire chain. The lures can take a beating around the bridge. The diving lips and natural painted sides will be cracked and chipped. Crankbaits, though, are usually mauled by the quarry that we seek rather than marred by concrete bridge pilings.

Speed cranking is a successful way to work the bridge pilings, but it is hard work. Speed cranking will not only wear out your arms and wrists, but it will also take its toll on your artificial baits. The fish can be there one day and gone the next. They'll move off the bridge to a nearby grassy point. That's where you'll also find the action on this lake.

I've found them schooling there often. I'll keep the electric motor on high speed and within a minute it's possible to cast to any surface-rising fish in the area. The grass shore adjacent to the bridge holds bass and lots of them. The largemouth often push schools of two-inch long threadfin shad against the thick cover. The bass will ambush the shad as they attempt to retreat back to deep water.

THE LITTLE LAKE

I'll usually work my crankbaits along the grass line from the bridge to a point 100 yards south of it in Little Lake Harris. I've found that as I move back and forth along this stretch I'll take healthy bass on each pass. Within 30 minutes, I have caught and released 10 largemouth on several occasions. They aren't usually big, 1-1/2 to three pounds, but they make for some fine action.

There are areas in Little Lake Harris other than the shoreline adjacent to the Howey Bridge that produce quality fishing. Specifically, the island grass beds in the lake's center and both structure drops and shoreline vegetation just off those shallows along the southern-most part of the lake are productive.

86

Big bass often inhabit the lily pads on the south end of Little Lake Harris.

The grassy east shoreline and the pad areas have produced heavy fish on topwater lures, minnow plugs and Berkley Power Worms. Bass will bed in the pads at Double Run during the spring. Casting the worms when the water is clear and flip them when the water is stained. Use a crankbait or vibrating plug on the thin, isolated pad areas on the outside of the main body of lilies.

On the east shore, a series of canals offer good spring bass fishing on plastic worms and vibrating plugs. Once you locate fish on this 20-square-mile lake, the key to catching several is to stay with them. The productive bass anglers will catch a bunch by going back and forth, once they've contacted fish in one area.

LAKE GRIFFIN'S COMEBACK

Twelve mile-long Lake Griffin is a narrow body of water which is more stained than many in the chain. The dark water and shoreline bulrush beds make this lake particularly good for utilizing the flippin' technique.

I've found several good areas on the lake's west shoreline above the prominent Picciola Point. The most productive areas are on several points along the west shoreline, around the Lake Griffin State Park and the mixed vegetation around Bird Island. Huge schools of largemouth actively feed on the rush points just north of Twin Palms Resort.

Wintering anglers and locals catch lots of big Griffin bass, and most regular lunker producers do so between 11 a.m. and 1 p.m. Several largemouth over 10 pounds have succumbed to grape

87

worms and spinnerbaits around the full moons. The grassy points at Picciola Point and Treasure Island Point are top bass producers on the lake.

Favorite bass areas also are the many canals that perforate the lake's shoreline. The Lake Yale Canal on the east shore and canals off the main lake's southwest corner provide good lunker angling. There is plenty of vegetation, such as hydrilla, lily pads and reeds, in the middle of the canals. Guides concentrate on the wide areas in the canals and on the scattered reeds. They toss plastic worms and spinnerbaits during low light levels for quick strikes.

The perimeter vegetation along the Yale Canal on the northeast side of the lake is productive for worm flippers. Others toss shallow-running crankbaits along the banks and to the middle of this seven-foot deep canal. Just south of the canal is Haines Creek. The bassin' is usually good at the mouth in the eight to 10 foot of water and on into the creek along its cattails and lily pads.

The locks on the chain offer good fishing in the spring and fall. The constant pumping to raise or lower water levels is a catalyst for feeding bass. The locks release huge amounts of water and, in the process, wounded baitfish. Successful anglers fishing the lock spillway overflow area employ heavy weights on their worm rigs to reach the bass.

Long gone are the huge rafts of pads, but fish-attracting reefs such as sunken brush piles have replaced that habitat. Marker buoys have been removed from the attractors, so a map and depth finder is generally required to find them. The lake went though a successful drawdown and revegetation project in the late 1980's.

Sunshine Options

The sunshine bass fishery in the chain is prospering due to the stocking efforts by the Game and Fresh Water Fish Commission. In the previous four years, close to one-half million sunshine bass have been stocked in Lake Harris.

Sunshine bass are taken year-round, but they prefer to school and feed vigorously in open water during the cooler months of the year. They will take live bait, such as minnows, quite readily, as well as strike small spinners, shad-resembling plugs and jigs. Trolling is the most effective way to locate these schools. Fishing live bait in the spring holes is the best method during the hotter months. Fishing with bait minnows at night with a bright light as a fish attractor is popular and productive. The fish are more active then.

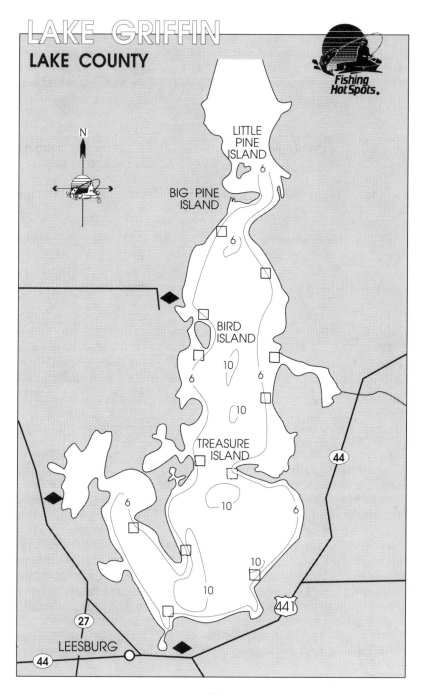

LAKE GRIFFIN

LAKE COUNTY

Fishing Hot Spots

N

LITTLE PINE ISLAND

6

BIG PINE ISLAND

6

BIRD ISLAND

10

6   6

10

TREASURE ISLAND

44

6

10   6

6

10

10

441

27

44

LEESBURG

44

89

For jump fishing the schools that are feeding on shad, minnow plugs and chugger topwater lures are tops. Either one of the twosome with a small white jig rigged as a trailer one foot behind the plug can be especially effective. Once the sunshine bass sound in the depths, jigging spoons are a good choice.

LAKE DETAILS

Lake Harris (13,788 acres) is almost 27-1/2 square miles of bass-filled water which stretches 9-1/2 miles in one direction and 11 in another (at the widest point). Lake Griffin (16,505 acres) has 27 miles of shoreline, a maximum depth of 16 feet and an average depth of 10. Little Lake Harris (2,739 acres) averages around 10 feet deep.

The water flowing out of the north end of Lake Griffin are the headwaters of the Oklawaha River. From the chain's outlet, the Oklawaha River flows north. Most of the portion of the river between Griffin and Highway 40 has been altered from the natural river course and channeled into canals.

Much of the flow into the Upper Oklawaha River Basin originates from the Palatlakaha River subbasin which flows into Lake Harris. The Clermont Chain of Lakes drains into Lake Harris through the Palatlakaha River. Lake Harris drains into Lake Eustis (on the eastern portion of the chain) through the Dead River, and Lake Eustis is connected to Lake Griffin by Haines Creek.

Several springs in the western section of the Harris Chain also contribute to the water inflow. Bugg Spring, located southwest of Leesburg and north of Okahumpka, discharges into Lake Harris via Helena Run. Blue Spring, located on the south shore of Lake Harris, discharges through a 125-foot long culvert into the lake, and Holiday Springs discharges into Lake Harris via a quarter mile meandering run.

Virtually all the surface water flow is regulated by water control structures in Haines Creek and the Oklawaha River. Annual fluctuation on most of the chain usually does not exceed two feet. The lock structures have dampened the natural periodic fluctuations in lake stages and stream discharges. As a result, the lakes function hydrologically as managed reservoirs rather than natural water bodies.

There are two navigation locks on this part of the chain, one at Haines Creek between Lake Eustis and Lake Griffin, and the other

The canal systems on the Harris Chain are productive largemouth areas.

just north of Lake Griffin on the Oklawaha River. All canals on the chain are posted as "no wake" areas, and boats in Haines Creek off Lake Griffin and Dead River off Lake Harris must come off a plane and idle by boats not under power. The heaviest boat traffic on the chain is in those two waterways.

Both Little Lake Harris and Lake Harris are relatively clear, while Lake Griffin is one of the most fertile lakes in the entire chain. A drawdown of Lake Griffin was conducted in 1984 in an attempt to restore the vegetation, soil and fishery. Unfortunately, in 1987, the resurging vegetation community was mostly eliminated by a herbicide treatment.

RAMP/GUIDE DETAILS

There are several ramps on this section of the Harris Chain of Lakes which encompasses Lake Griffin north of Leesburg, and Lake Harris and Little Lake Harris south of Leesburg. On Lake Griffin, there are three. On the north west side near Lake Griffin

Resort is a small ramp with fee parking. On the west side off Highway 27-441 is the beautiful Lake Griffin State Recreation Area, and on the south side off Highway 441 is the popular Herlong Park ramp.

Lake Harris also has three public ramps, two of which are on the northwest side off Highway 44 in the town of Leesburg. One is located behind Pat Thomas Memorial Field and the other is found off Lakeshore Drive across from Venetian Gardens. On the west side of Lake Harris off Highway 27 is the Singletary Park facility which provides a double concrete boat ramp. Little Lake Harris has two rough, unimproved ramps; one is on the northwest side just south of the Highway 19 bridge and the other on the east side off Highway 561 in the town of Astatula.

For information on guide service on Lakes Griffin and Harris, contact Jim Bitter's Professional Guide Booking Service, Sportsmans Headquarters, 411 E. North Blvd., Leesburg, FL 32748 or Phone (904) 787-5181.

9

EAST HARRIS CHAIN OVERLOOKED WATERS

MANY AN ANGLER has fished the Harris Chain of Lakes near Leesburg, but often the lakes on the eastern side of the chain have been overlooked. Armadas flock to "more famous" waters around Central Florida that yield less activity. These largemouth bass waters, also known as the Oklawaha Chain of Lakes, are among the best bass waters in the state for both quantity and quality.

There are nine principal lakes in the chain, of which eight are interconnected. The six lakes in the eastern section include Lakes Apopka, Beauclair, Carlton, Dora, Eustis and Yale. All, except Lake Apopka, provide excellent bass fishing. Moving water is a key to finding concentrations of bass in this section of the chain. Find currents due to runoffs or strong winds, and you'll probably discover bass feeding. Check the canals, areas where the lake "necks down," all inlets (or outlets) and all downwind points in these waters.

The fishing pressure is light on this side of the chain, and there's plenty of largemouth action available.

The Dead River, which is a one mile long connection between Lakes Harris (on the western section of the chain) and Eustis, has many fields of pads which make for good fishing when boat traffic is minimal. The numerous lily pads in five feet of water near mouth of the river as it enters Eustis is particularly productive. Guides will normally flip or cast plastic worms to the cover.

Lake Eustis

Lake Eustis itself is a large body of water covering some 19 square miles. While not as popular as some other chain waters, this lake does produce a lot of bass. One of the shallowest lakes in the chain, Eustis grass patches along the southeastern and east shorelines are worth working due to their proximity to good structure. Lunker bass hang out in these stretches, as well as around the deep water docks and near mouths of numerous canals on the lake.

Crankbaits, worms, and Rat-L-Traps retrieved near the grass beds at the canal entrances are usually successful. The mouth of Haines Creek in the northwest corner of the lake is a great spot for stringers of largemouth and while this area is lightly fished, weekend boat traffic can shut off the fishing action.

On the north side of the lake, the Goose Prairie lily pads and the canals into Grand Island are good areas to flip a plastic worm or cast a spinnerbait. The depth in the canals varies from four to 10 feet, and those lures and crankbaits can be effective in early spring for pre-spawners. The grassy shoal areas along the eastern shoreline and the deep holes off them are productive too. Guides fish the scattered docks and cypress trees in early spring and flip the maidencane for bass the remainder of the year.

Haines Creek runs from Lake Eustis westerly for about nine miles where it enters Lake Griffin. This stretch of narrow waterway with offshoot canals and dead end channels is my favorite area on the chain for scrappy spring time bass. Heavy shoreline cover in the form of brush and overhanging trees create largemouth habitat that is hard to top.

A friend and I once put together a 35 pound stringer of largemouth from the narrow creek to win a boat tournament, and I've had a warm spot in my heart for it since. We were flipping and casting plastic worms to the variety of cover along the waterway: brush, limbs, grass, cattails and reeds. The area above the Haines Creek lock has numerous small islands and canals, and it has historically been one of the best places on the chain to catch largemouth. When the lock has been opened for boat traffic, the moving current seems to turn on the bass.

The mouth of the numerous canals off Eustis are often productive, and that includes Dora Canal when there is current moving through it. You may catch schooling bass about 50 to 100 yards from the mouth of the canal. For the best bet, spray cast a Rat-L-Trap during late summer and fall months.

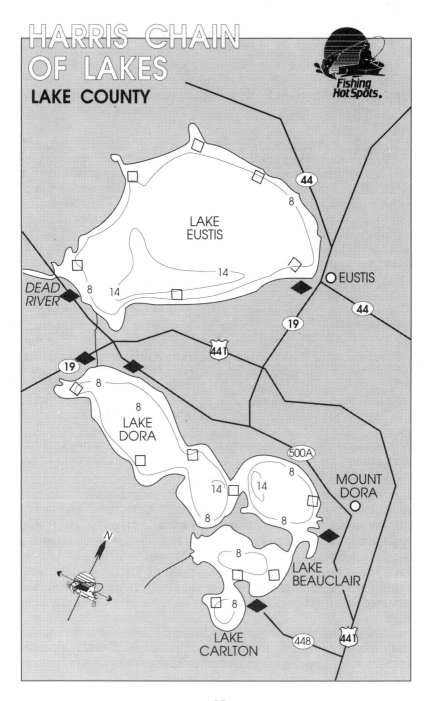

HARRIS CHAIN OF LAKES
LAKE COUNTY

Fishing Hot Spots.

44

8

LAKE EUSTIS

14

DEAD RIVER
8   14

EUSTIS

44

19

441

19

8

8

LAKE DORA

500A

14   14

8

8

MOUNT DORA

8

LAKE BEAUCLAIR

N

8

LAKE CARLTON

448   441

LAKE DORA

This lake offers more prime bass waters which are cypress stained. The Dora Canal itself is a beautifully natural creek through huge cypress trees between lakes Eustis and Dora. Despite the unspoiled scenery, boat traffic prevents most serious fishing attempts.

The northern shoreline grass in Lake Dora, just east of the canal, is a favorite spot of bass pluggers and wormers, Several docks, ramps, etc., provide bass breaks in the structure which create numerous points of vegetation along a three-mile stretch. The mile-long stretch of docks along the southern shore at Mount Dora offers excellent bass fishing in the summer months.

Lake Dora is among the first on the chain to turn on with the spring's first warm spell. Flippin' the thick reeds is a successful technique when the action heats up. Spinnerbait fishing is also a very productive tactic for bass that are buried in scattered maidencane grass, reeds and lily pads emerging from about six feet of water. Use a white spinnerbait and work it by "slow rolling" it deep into the grass.

Squirrel Point and Holler's Point are grassy areas in the "Narrows" section of Dora that produce lots of lunkers. Flip plastic worms into the cattails, scattered maidencane or lily pads for bass action. Fish the grassy Wooten Park area and the stick-ups along the eastern shoreline.

The cattails and brush at the mouth of Beauclair Canal are a good springtime area for fat trophy bass. Crankbaits and spinnerbaits both take their share of the bass here, as do purple or dark grape wigglers. Flip the plastic worms into the brush and toss the hard baits to the patches of vegetation.

LAKE BEAUCLAIR

Just south of Lake Dora through a 'cut' at the lake's east end lies the top lunker lake in the chain. Lake Beauclair is a murky, shallow watershed that's loaded with trophy fish. The mouths at each end of the lake are productive, as is the point on the southeast shore. The stretch of wooden docks on the east shoreline are productive flippin' areas, as are the cattails around the Trimble Park area.

Good structure near the lake's center offers top fishing for anglers with depth recorders on this lightly fished water. Springs at the back of some of the canals off Beauclair offer some excellent

Rat-L-Traps fished outside of the grass edges on the chain's lakes are usually effective.

lunker bass angling. The pH level in such waters is prime for an early spring spawn, probably the first on the chain each year.

The Apopka-Beauclair Canal running south out of Lake Beauclair may be a surprise to many. The smaller canals off the main canal provide scrappy largemouth and produce occasional stringers of big bass. The water depths vary greatly, as do the cover and water clarity from one to another. There are plenty of docks to fish and a perimeter of maidencane and cattails in the canal system. Some canals are clear, inviting topwater action, and others are prime for flippin'.

A swimming worm can be especially effective. A six-inch purple wiggler with glo-pink tail, strung on a 2/0 straight-shank bait hook, is connected via a 14" leader to one (or two) ball bearing swivels. The worm rig twists as it is retrieved from the canal's often heavy shoreline cover.

The cattails on the western side of tiny Lake Carlton offer excellent flippin' water. The water has a green tint and visibility of less than a foot at the edge of the cattails, so locals who flip the plastic worms in the springtime usually do well. They often use a 1/2 ounce weight and peg it above a worm or plastic crayfish replica.

LAKE APOPKA

Historically, Lake Apopka was widely known as one of the best bass lakes in the state...until the 1950's. A poorly developed vegetation community and extensive pollution from agriculture devastated the bass fishing in the early 60's. Muck farms along the canal were blamed for the deterioration then, and the farms still exist today. Cattle grazing and natural foliage, though, has replaced much of the bare banks that used to exist.

Today, bass fishing opportunities are minimal in the 47-square mile Lake Apopka. The pollution which virtually killed the lake is slowly being "filtered out". Angling has not substantially come back yet, but the restoration continues. The highly degraded lake was initially stocked with almost one half million bass fingerlings in 1982, but the fishery failed due to a lack of suitable water quality and habitat.

Those conditions changed, and in 1990, the Game and Fresh Water Fish Commission completed its largest stocking of largemouth in any water ever, when one million bass fry were placed in Lake Apopka. The effort should enhance the bass fishery that has been non-existent for many years.

About the only area on the lake offering any bass fishing currently is Gourd Neck Springs. The bass are often located on the outside edges of the spring in three feet of water or on the drop which tapers to 10 feet. Locals will fish Texas-rigged plastic worms around the boiling water, or around the sunken brush in the spring boil area.

LAKE YALE

This overlooked fishery, off highway 452 near the small town of Umatilla, is the only one in the chain that is not interconnected for boat traffic. It is accessible only by ramp. The clearest water of the Harris Chain is found in Lake Yale, and as a result, vegetation growth can be abundant. Shoreline grass beds, hydrilla, numerous docks and lily pads enhance the bass action here.

Anglers should check out the lily pads along the Yale Canal creek bed. Plastic worms and topwater baits are effective there in the spring and summer months. Rabbit Island Cove offers clear water and lily pads in five feet of water. The bass love this area and that just off Marsh Park in the lake's southern corner. There are some holes in the bottom that are over 24 feet deep.

Sunken islands lying in 15 feet of water yield bass to those equipped with sonar and the ability to find them. In fact, the hard bottom topography on Yale offers some of the most unique situations found in Central Florida. Hydrilla growing on the humps, ridges and submerged islands attracts the bass. Successful anglers will fish a Carolina-rigged worm down the drops. Others tight-line shiners on the bottom for bass action.

The best patterns on Lake Yale, though, are topwater plugs fished in the open pockets, plastic frogs fished across the top of the pads and plastic worms crawled along the root areas of the pads. Topwater plugs worked over the hydrilla, coontail and scattered brush piles are effective all seasons as well. Yale has three fish attractors which also attract bass, and some productive bass anglers troll crankbaits outside of the weedline.

Sun Shine On Me

Sunshine bass fishing doesn't get any better than it does on Lake Yale, particularly in one hole about 30 feet deep. The hole seems to be one of the reasons for the sunshine's success in the lake. Four pounders are common, and they range to around ten pounds. The hybrid striped bass or sunshine bass is not limited to Lake Yale either. In fact, Lake Eustis is also a sunshine hotspot.

Throughout the Harris Chain, sunshine bass are the stocking focus. In the past three years, almost 100,000 sunshine bass fingerlings have been stocked in Lakes Dora and Eustis. In Lake Apopka, over one million sunshines have been stocked, and in little Lake Carlton, over 20,000 sunshine bass have been introduced in the same period.

Sunshine bass, a cross between a striped bass male and a white bass female, roam a different area than largemouth and generally do not compete with them for forage. They travel in schools and are extremely aggressive. The fish have a definite food preference and tops on the list is shad. They prefer the bite-size threadfin shad that frequent open water.

Structure fishing patterns developed with sonar can be established and either casting or trolling techniques can be productive most times of the year. When sunshine bass are schooling and popping the shad at the top, then surface tactics can be used to advantage. They have a lure preference for white, silver or gold colored baits. For casting, Threadfin Shad plugs and bucktail or maribou jigs are hard to beat. White or yellow grubs are deadly as are the heavy slab spoons and tail spinner baits.

Trolling favorites such as Hellbenders, Deep Runners and Bombers are the usual fare, and a fast retrieve or troll has proved most productive. Light weight spoons and spinners, as well as top water plugs, can be productive in a thrashing school of surface feeders. A dynamic duo which is successful on hybrids consists of a Deep Diver and a small white jig attached about two feet behind the lure. A final productive method to take sunshine bass is by drifting minnows or other forage fish over structure.

LAKE DETAILS

Lake Apopka with 30,671 acres is the second largest lake in Florida and the largest body of water in the Harris chain. Lakes Yale (4,042 acres) and Eustis (7,806 acres) both have water depths exceeding 20 feet and an average around 12 feet. Lake Dora (4,475 acres) and tiny Lake Carlton (382 acres) average around 10 feet deep, and Lakes Beauclair (1,111 acres) and Apopka both average seven to eight feet deep.

Navigation through the Yale Canal is blocked off to boat traffic, but there are two navigation locks on the chain. The one with heaviest use is the Haines Creek Lock between Lake Eustis and Lake Griffin. The other, the lock between Lake Apopka and Lake Beauclair, is seldom used. Precipitation, evaporation and the locks control the chain's water level.

All canals on the chain are posted as "no wake" areas, and they are enforced. Additionally, boats in Haines Creek and Dead River must come off a plane and idle by boats not under power. When moving through Haines Creek and other interconnecting waterways, the regulations may slow you considerably. The heaviest boat traffic on the chain is in Haines Creek, the Dora Canal and the Dead River.

This chain forms the headwaters of the Oklawaha River, and at least 38 tributaries generate the stream over its course. Most of the flow through the eastern portion of the chain originates from Gourd Neck Springs, located in the southwest corner of Lake Apopka. It is considered the headwaters of the Oklawaha Chain of Lakes.

Water from Gourd Neck Springs flows north through Lake Apopka into Lake Beauclair through the Apopka-Beauclair Canal. Lake Beauclair drains directly into Lake Dora, which drains into Lake Eustis through the Dora Canal. Lake Eustis via Haines Creek and Lake Yale through the Yale-Griffin Canal drain into Lake Griffin.

Flowing water through the many creeks and canals connecting the chain of lakes is an excellent place to employ an attractant on a plastic worm.

RAMP/GUIDE DETAILS

There are many public launch facilities on the eastern Harris Chain. They include the Dora Canal park ramp between Lakes Dora and Eustis off Highway 19 and Lake Harris Drive, the Tavares Recreational Park ramps on the south side of Lake Eustis off Highway 441 and the newly renovated Lakeshore Drive boat ramp in the town of Eustis on the east side of Lake Eustis off Highway 19. On Lake Dora, there are two public ramps; Wooten Park on the northwest side off Highway 452 in the town of Tavares and Gilbert Park in the town of Mount Dora on the east side off Highway Old 441.

The Trimble Park ramp is on the south side of Lake Beauclair off Highway 448, and on the east side of the Apopka-Beauclair Canal off the same highway is a small park ramp. Access from the latter is provided to either Lake Apopka south through a lock or north directly to Lake Beauclair. There are several ramps on Lake Apopka. On the east side off Highway 437 is Magnolia Park, on the south side off Highway 438 is the Winter Garden city park ramp,

101

and on the west side off Highway 455 in the town of Monteverde is an unimproved ramp suitable for trucks and 4-wheel drive vehicles.

Access to the other Harris Chain lakes from Lake Yale is not possible, but there are two public ramps on the lake. On the south side off Highway 452 is the Marsh Park ramp. On the northeast side off Highway 450 and Yale Hammock Road is the Lake Yale Boat Ramp.

For information on guides, contact Jim Bitter's Professional Guide Booking Service, Sportsmans Headquarters, 411 E. North Blvd., Leesburg, FL 32748 or Phone (904) 787-5181.

10

CLERMONT CHAIN ATTRACTIONS

THE GRASSLINE PERIMETER of Lake Minnehaha is often productive, as it was on the day a friend and I caught 12 largemouth in about one hour's time. Our plastic worms were chewed up, as the active bass charged most of the offerings like it was their last meal. It wasn't; we released them all.

Such fishing is little known on this chain of 13 interconnected lakes in Lake County off highway 27 near the town of Clermont. The clean-water chain totals over 8,600 surface acres and varies in water color, depth and surrounding terrain. The waters of many, particularly those with cypress tree perimeters, are tannin-stained. But those chain lakes without the cypress buffer zone are very clear, and that poses problems for bass anglers used to tossing 20 pound test line.

This picturesque chain of lakes in the citrus groves of Lake County offers numerous bass opportunities.

Grass points, several small islands and huge cypress tree knees on Minnehaha are attractive to largemouth. I can't recall seeing a more "bassy-looking" grass line on any Central Florida lake; it's postcard beauty for an avid angler. The vegetated edges of coves and the holes, cuts and pockets inside the grassline often produce bass. Other dropoffs down to 30 feet occasionally yield fish in the temperature extremes of summer and winter.

The 2,264-acre Minnehaha has more feeder creeks and canals coming into (or leaving) it than any other chain lake. Such areas, particularly when the water is flowing, are excellent largemouth havens. At times, the water movement will vary, so it is wise to check out all the inlets and the exit before making that first cast.

Most of the veteran bass anglers fish 12 to 15 pound test line on Minnehaha -- it garners more strikes. If a big bass becomes entangled in the weeds, it doesn't make sense to "horse" the fish in on 12 pound test. Steady pressure may allow the fish to swim free of the grass clump, but, more often than not, you have to move to the fish and try to free it at the entanglement.

Boaters can move from Lake Louisa on the south end through the chain to Lake Cherry, located on the northern end. Above Lake Cherry, a dam impedes your progress. Running from one end of the chain to the other takes about 45 minutes. Highway 50 cuts across the picturesque chain, leaving Lakes Minneola, Hiawatha, Wilson and Cherry to the north. On the south side of the highway are Lakes Minnehaha, Palatlakaha, Winona, Hattie, Susan, Louisa and Crescent.

NORTH OF HIGHWAY 50

Lake Minneola (which means "sparkling water") is a gin-clear 1,888-acre lake that usually stays that way during normal to low water conditions. It has several deep holes along the southeast corner, and a good depth finder will help you locate them. For those non-boaters wanting to try the lake, a long T-shaped pier is located on the south shore. Check out the dredge holes off the lake's docks with a Rat-L-Trap or Carolina-rigged worm.

One of my favorite spots on Minneola is a grass line along the western shore. I have caught several largemouth from the weed edge and from just offshore of that. Top choices of baits are Texas- and Carolina-rigged plastic worms and deep-running crankbaits.

The twisting Palatlakaha River leaves Minneola and heads through a sawgrass flats area to tiny Lake Wilson (32 acres). The river was named by the Creek Indians and pronounced Palat-la-ka-ha. It means "big area of swamps and hammocks." The most productive spots along this tributary are at its mouths on both lakes. The outer bends of the river are deeper and also hold largemouth, particularly when the water is flowing fairly rapidly.

The 396-acre Cherry with a variety of pads, reeds, grass beds and deep holes, is one of the best bass producers. Tournaments have been won on the lake, and topwater plugs and jerkbaits often are effective there. Lake Hiawatha, located just north of the highway 50 bridge, is a 48-acre body of water off Lake Minneola that many anglers pass through.

The beautiful cypress trees lining Lake Minnehaha are often productive during low light situations.

SOUTH OF HIGHWAY 50

Lakes Minnehaha and Louise are the giants of the chain. Louise, at 3,364 acres is also the shallowest. In fact, knee-deep water 100 feet offshore exists in some areas. It averages only about 10 feet in the middle, and unless you fish one of the fish attractors or drift-fish the bottom in open water, the pickings are slim.

Those anglers who want to cast to the banks can try the west and southern shorelines, or the feeder streams (Little Creek and Big Creek) entering the lake on the south side. Also check out the cypress trees on the north end of the lake. The clear water makes Lake Louise an excellent night fishing venture, although few try it.

The 101-acre Lake Palatlakaha, named for the river that binds the chain, lies to the north of Minnehaha and just south of the highway 50 bridge. It has produced some giant bass exceeding 13 pounds. So has Lake Susan, another small lake (81 acres) that's south of Lake Minnehaha. Susan is a beautiful tannin-stained lake that has produced a larger average size bass than many of the others in the chain. Check out the fish attractor located in the south cove area.

Lakes Willaimie (6 acres) and Little Lake Hattie (3 acres) are little more than wide spots in the creek going from Minnehaha into Lake Crescent. The 143-acre Crescent with a mixture of vegetation along its perimeter is a good place to toss spinnerbaits and soft plastic jerk worms. Hooks Point on Lake Winona is another productive spot for bassmen tossing shallow-running fare. The 75-acre lake off the north side of Minnehaha also offers good dock fishing and several holes down to 25 feet deep for the structure fishermen to search out.

CANAL MAGIC

The waterways between lakes on this chain can also be productive. Most of them are lined with grasses and have overhanging trees and submerged brush below. Many have deep holes that have collected additional structure, and that attracts forage and bass. Check out the depths with sonar for such a find as you cruise through them. Pay special attention to the mouths of each creek or canal -- you'll find very productive dropoffs there.

When winds are blowing across the larger lakes, the waterways offer some protection. While some are short and open, others are quite long and offer tree-lined banks. One of the best ways to escape white caps on the chain is to consult a map and head for either the longest creek that runs perpendicular to the wind or for the waterway with the most turns and twists.

FISH ATTRACTIONS

There are many man-made bass attractors on the chain, in addition to its great natural habitat. The Florida Game and Freshwater Fish Commission fish attractor construction crew recently refurbished 14 hardwood brush attractors.

Two refurbished attractors in Cherry Lake, the older one in Lake Minneola and a new attractor in front of Lake Minneola's public fishing pier, are all productive bass hotspots. The brush is anchored to the bottom in an upright position and covers approximately one quarter acre at each location. Marker buoys are placed at the center of each site to aid fishermen in finding the attractors.

"The hardwood brush attractors start drawing bass to the area quickly and continue to be effective for approximately four years," says Gib Owen, a Commission fisheries biologist. "The best fishing results can be obtained by anchoring about 50 feet away from the buoy, so that the edges and center of the attractor can be fished."

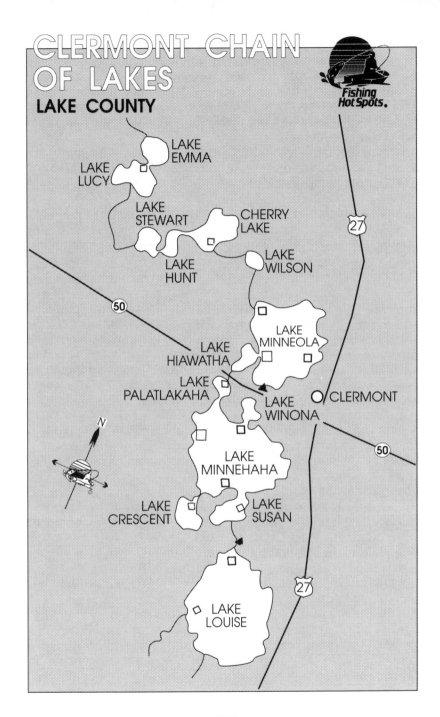

CLERMONT CHAIN OF LAKES

LAKE COUNTY

LAKE EMMA

LAKE LUCY

LAKE STEWART

CHERRY LAKE

LAKE HUNT

LAKE WILSON

27

50

LAKE HIAWATHA

LAKE MINNEOLA

LAKE PALATLAKAHA

LAKE WINONA

CLERMONT

50

N

LAKE MINNEHAHA

LAKE CRESCENT

LAKE SUSAN

LAKE LOUISE

27

Fishing Hot Spots.

"Problems develop when people anchor within 50 feet of the buoy because anchors catch on the brush and drag it out of its proper configuration," Owen said. "This decreases the effectiveness of the site to attract sport fish, and the anchors tend to break off pieces of the brush, which shortens the life of the attractors considerably."

Several other waters on the Clermont Chain have the productive attractors. Lake Minnehaha has four, Lake Louisa has three and Lake Crescent has two attractors. Lakes Susan and Palatlakaha each have one.

There are public ramps on the canal at the north end of Lake Louisa and on the south end of Lake Minneola. A couple of fishing resorts/camps also offer excellent launch areas. A good map of this area would be helpful in driving around the chain; there are many roads and turns to see all the lakes by land (or by water).

TACTICS, LURES & BAIT

When it is hot, largemouth in these predominantly shallow, natural waters resort to hiding out in or under the cover that's available to them. Aquatic vegetation in the chain's lakes must be thick to attract a bass. There is plenty of that, and according to my good friend Dave Burkhardt who lives on the chain, the largemouth are usually active in the late afternoons.

Dave, an executive with Classic Manufacturing, uses these waters as proving grounds for testing various plastic products that his company produces. In fact, the Classic Jerk Worm met rave reviews due to its success on several of the chain's waters. The Sticky Worm was also field tested and developed from response generated by the chain's bass.

Man-made structures, such as the Commission attractors and numerous docks and piers, also seem to act as magnets during warm weather. Docks exist on most Clermont Chain lakes, and they hold more bass during the month of July than at any other time of the year. Piers, pilings and other structural handyman work provide a cooler, darker habitat for forage and their less mobile predators.

Plastic worms rigged either Texas-style or in a "swimming" configuration are preferred by many chain bassmen fishing the wood structures. Crankbaits and vibrating plugs which resemble threadfin shad are also used by the careful casters to entice their share of battling largemouth from the docks.

Some of the smaller waters on the Clermont chain are ideal for a small boat and light tackle.

All of the chain's waters harbor 10-pound bass, and all have development on their shores. Smart anglers will concentrate on the wood structures, tributary mouths and vegetation that abounds on the chain.

11

FORTY SOMETHING
BASS HOLES

I WAS ADMIRING the wood duck boxes acting as sentries over the small lagoons within an expanse of emergent grass. My spinnerbait had landed softly in the shallow water beside a piling holding one of the specially-constructed waterfowl houses, and I had begun the retrieve.

The wake moving toward my lure's path caught my eye just before the strike. The bait was approaching the cut into the pocket when the fish seized the opportunity for an easy "meal." I set back on the rod as a bass bulged the surface and quickly headed into the grass.

Overlooked lakes and ponds along highways 40, 42 and 44 are largemouth hotspots.

"Got a big one," I told my partner, as he turned to view the commotion. "She's buried up though."

A tight line kept me in touch with the fish's movements as it struggled with a ball of grass. I pressured her out of the grassy hangup and she came to the surface, rolled, and again swam into the dense grass cover a few feet closer to the boat. Again, the huge largemouth buried herself momentarily, causing now more than a little concern on my part.

I swiveled my seat to a better position for the continuing battle in open water. The 10-pound-plus bass again surfaced before apparently feeling free to take off. The open water with no encumbrances was excuse enough for her to charge off at full throttle. The ten pound test line, obviously frayed by the encounters with dense vegetation, popped before my drag could kick in.

I had a sick feeling in my stomach from losing that fish. I have been very fortunate in landing most of the larger bass I've tangled with. The only other "big fish that got away" story that I can remember in the past 12 years or so was not even a largemouth bass. The 20-pound peacock bass straightened out four treble hook points on a large topwater plug and pulled free after a five minute battle.

This fish, although hooked on light spinning tackle, was in open water and should have been different, so I blamed myself. My partner, Bing McClellan, understood my frustration, as I stared at the two beefy baitcasting outfits laying beside me. Each one had 20 pound test monofilament line, durable enough to survive most grassy entanglements. I had tied the 3/8 ounce Tornado spinnerbait on the light outfit with some hesitation when I did it. The results proved the concern was valid.

That giant bass was the only strike that we had in two hours of fishing Lake Dorr's grass perimeter. The small lake north of Bing's new residence in Eustis is an isolated one. Few houses or other shoreline developments exist, so the casting cover is natural and abundant.

OUT OF THE WAY FISHING

"This area's got a lot of little-fished waters that are loaded with fish," he told me. "Many have 10 and 12 pounders, and very few fishermen even know of some. The locals often stick to the Harris Chain, the big waters, but I like the small, out-of-the-way places. My boat is specifically equipped for them, and I just don't like the crowds that are sometimes found on bigger waters."

His 15-foot stick-steered bass boat painted in camouflaged colors is set up for the small water soul. Everything is close by and can be handled from the front seat. A 50-horsepower motor pushes the vessel quickly from one shore to another when needed, and his trolling motor handles positioning while fishing.

Showers preceding an approaching front skirted us for the most part, but our rain gear was employed periodically. Bing wanted to show me another small chain of eight lakes about 20 minutes away from Lake Dorr, so we put the boat back on the trailer during a lull in the showers. We pulled into the county ramp at the first lake in the Holly Chain located just off S.R. 450 and launched. Motoring through the chain is a scenic experience. The lakes vary in topography and habitat-type, but the cover in each should be exciting to most bass anglers.

112

Bing McClellan finds bass and solitude on many of the small waters around Eustis.

Each of the small lakes in the chain has emergent grass beds and some are surrounded by cattails and rushes. Others have irregular shorelines with numerous pockets of lily pads and pickerel weed. All have bass.

We had just shut off the engine in the "water ski" lake and made a couple of casts when Bing put the first bass in the boat. Four or five casts later, he caught and released another one pound largemouth. The pads along the lake seemed to invite our casts, so we paid no attention to the powerful ski boat that moved off shore toward us.

The MasterCraft idled through the ski buoys, past the ski jump and actually asked us if their skiing the slalom course would bother our fishing. We told them to go ahead. Neither of us had ever been so courteously approached by water skiers. We were definitely taken aback by the query. While we marveled over such on-the-water etiquette, the storm began to intensify.

Bing caught two more small largemouth, before we ducked into a smaller lake with lightning and thunder surrounding us. The electrical storm veered off to the east, fortunately, but our luck on staying relatively dry soon ran out. A downpour began and after 20 minutes, few dry spots existed under my rain gear. With our afternoon casting cut short, we headed for the ramp.

BOMBS OVERHEAD, BASS BELOW

Lake Dorr, which lies off highway 19 just north of highway 42 and the town of Umatilla in Lake County, was where Bing had one week earlier successfully battled a 7-1/2 pound largemouth to the boat. The 1,533-acre lake is good for year around bass action, according to the life-long fisherman. Several oft-times productive swampy areas exist under the overhanging trees found along the shore.

There is plenty of bass forage in the lake, including bream, various minnows and large native shiners. The only other boat Bing and I saw that rainy morning, in fact, was a couple of canepole fisherman trying to catch shiners for use later as bait. Two ramps are accessible on the west side of the lake about three miles north of the highway's intersection with S.R. 42. The lake has a state-developed recreation site on its northwest corner.

Another fan of Lake Dorr is guide Bob Stonewater of nearby DeLand. The strict conservationist fishes it and other small waters in the area when the St. Johns River is most crowded, such as on weekends. He believes that the average size bass caught on shiners from the lake is almost five pounds. He has caught and released numerous bass between six and 10 in the lake.

The pockets back in the grass are productive for Bob, as well as the boat docks that exist on the south side of Dorr. He has taken more big fish off wood than any other structure, the guide contends. The docks there are surrounded by grass and in three to six feet of water, ideal for trophy bass. The ones that extend to the deepest dropoff are the most productive for his shiners.

About the only discomforting thought about Lake Dorr is that it lies just south of the U.S. Navy Bombing Range. That means air traffic can be noisy at times, and, in fact, on the morning that I accompanied Bing to the lake, a couple of high-tech bombers circled over the lake as we were thinking of changing waters. The loud roar of the jets was something we could very well do without, and we decided to.

DIAS LANDINGS AND ATTRACTIONS

Lake Dias is a beautiful clear, stained lake that lies off S.R. 11 about nine miles north of highway 44 in Deland. The air traffic there, at least on the day Bob Stonewater and I fished the lake, was confined to two sea planes that landed in the middle of the lake twice and quickly took off each time. Our day with the fish was an exciting one, though. Two largemouth of four pounds each and another small one convinced me of the lake's potential.

But I'll never forget my experience when I hooked and eventually lost the largest freshwater fish of my life. The fish was one-foot wide across its back and almost six feet long. The alligator gar was truly a monster with a 16-inch bill full of menacing teeth. It struck a live shiner, and I knew when I set the hook, it was a giant.

My seven-foot heavy action rod with oversized bait casting reel and 40 pound test Trilene Big Game line seemed formidable, but the fish swam where it wanted. Fortunately, that was toward the boat where the battle continued. Bob forgot all about the net when the fish surfaced next to the boat. That fish in the boat alive, we knew then, would destroy everything.

When it saw its predicament at the gunwale, it took off, but I snubbed it short. It quickly reversed its course back to the boat, and I again tried to control its direction. That's when it happened, and I'll never forget it.

Six feet of giant gar shot straight up out of the water clearing the surface. The tarpon-like leap for freedom worked and the hook pulled free at that moment. The jump was as impressive as any I'd seen a big fish make. It came skyward with body twisting and gill plates shaking and fell back tail-first. The largest freshwater fish that either Bob or I had seen in action swam off.

Bob's clients have caught hundreds of largemouth bass over 10 pounds and one even landed a 42-pound catfish, but this fish was big and mean. We estimated it weighed at least 50 pounds, but neither of us have actually seen gar of those proportions weighed.

BASS ATTRACTORS

Several small schooling bass surfaced periodically, but we opted to fish our 6- to 12- inch native shiners for a chance at one of Dias' big largemouth. We fished the two fish attractors and caught fish from both places. Bob has found them to be very productive from early spring through late fall when larger fish move off the heavily-vegetated shoreline during high sun times.

"Those attractors have made a big difference here because there isn't much deep water structure," he told me. "You can use shiners, crankbaits or worms around these attractors and usually catch fish. If one is not working, the other will."

Dias is about one-half mile wide by two miles long with a submerged bar or hump midway along the north shoreline. The lake has a sandy hard bottom with some lily pads, fallen trees along some banks and a perimeter of sawgrass. It produces plenty of bass over eight pounds. Bob knows of two lake largemouth that exceeded 14 pounds and heard of another even larger. Trolling shiners along the shoreline has been responsible for many of those trophies.

"We like to put two shiners out under corks and another on a free-line when trolling," says Bob. "Set the bobbers at different depths to cover the whole area, and then work in and out in a weaving pattern to cover all depths. You'll get the bigger fish out away from the bank where the darkness of the water lies at three to six feet. The trophies will lay out there just past that sun penetration."

Other Trophy Waters

Not too far away, right in the city limits of Umatilla, is Lake Umatilla, a small meandering waterway in pretty rolling hills. A small, but good launch ramp provides access to the lake. The waters with plenty of sharp dropoffs and maximum depths of 23 feet are also overlooked by area bass anglers.

Locals have caught several trophy-size largemouth from the "seemingly" urban lake which, in fact, has almost half of its shore without development. Those stretches of natural shoreline vegetation are areas that Lake Umatilla's largemouth frequent. The bass tend to hang out in the standing cypress trees on the east and south sides. There are also pads on the lake that seem to concentrate the bass at times.

East of Umatilla just off S.R. 42 is Lake Norris, a cypress lake with perimeter of trees in three to four feet of water. There is a blackwater creek flowing into the lake and one leaving it. During high water conditions, bass can actually migrate into the lake from the Wekiva River, according to Stonewater. The spring-fed water is relatively clear, but the cypress have stained the waters. The lake produces bass for those bumping a worm or crankbait against the tree knees and roots.

Other area waters off highways 42 and 44 with good bass fishing are Lake Dolhousie, Blanchester, Nicatoon, Tracy and Norris. When the St. Johns and Oklawaha River systems are crowded on weekends, these little lakes are options that most

Lake Dias north of Deland offers guide Stonewater a variety of scenic shoreline cover to fish.

anglers enjoy. The fishing on most may be better than that found on the bigger waterways.

You don't normally find marinas on these small waterways, but most have an adequate launch ramp. Some may be suitable only for smaller craft, but that's fine for those "geared down" to the tiny waters.

12

ORLANDO AND TAMPA LAKES

LAKES ARE EVERYWHERE in the Greater Orlando area. Some say there are about 2,000 lakes, ponds and potholes. Any air flight reveals the abundant water that pockmarks the town's real estate. The glimmering waterways of Orlando are also apparent from the ground traffic pattern which seems to circle a lake every few blocks before continuing straight again.

Most of the waters in the bustling area, now known more for its man-made attractions than for its natural ones, offer public fishing. Very little pressure exists, however, due to the proximity of several larger "name" lakes.

The options in the two big Central Florida cities are numerous, and some are seldom fished.

The outstanding bass angling within city limits is mostly overlooked by local sportsmen's clubs, as well as the general fishing public. Beautiful lakes of 5 to 100 acres or more are often void of a single boat on a weekend. When I first moved to Orlando several years ago, I could lake-hop from one to another and cover five or six small waters in a day. That opportunity still exists today and the fishing is just as good.

On a recent trip to the city, some 50 minutes from where I now reside, I asked Doug Gilley to join me for some quick bass catching and photography. The professional angler suggested we try Lake Conway on the south side of Orlando. Within ten minutes, we had proof that city anglers don't have to trailer a boat far to enjoy bass action.

The lake, like others on the small chain, yields numerous largemouth. We caught six or seven bass on plastic worms in just a half hour and, through a culling process, selected the largest as our photography subjects. We left with plenty of time to take care of our other business that day.

The 1,767-acre Lake Conway is like most of the smaller potholes that pocket Orlando's landscape. It has a sandy bottom, fairly clear water and vegetation. Even though it's almost completely surrounded by homes, the lake has substantial aquatic habitat. The shorelines are shallow and wadeable. Best of all, it also has large bass.

Most of the city's waters grow big largemouth and plenty of them. Orlando's lakes generally have ideal pH and other water characteristics and are high in nutrients. That's reflected in the health of the bass and their forage. The abundant aquatic vegetation on most lakes provides predators with numerous baitfish and crustacean. Most city lake perimeters still sport a "weed fringe." Fairly rigid regulations see to that.

THE UNKNOWN TROPHY PRODUCERS

The lunkers that swim in the area's waters take a back seat to none. The occasional monster that is landed from one of the small lakes does make a "news splash" though. Few anglers in the city even had ever heard of 40-acre Lake Rose in western Orlando until a 17-1/2 pound largemouth was pulled from it in 1985. The private lake in west Orange County gave Mike Paule an experience he won't forget.

He was tossing a broken-back Rapala along a windblown weedline in eight feet of water when the monster hit. The lure was cast to the sawgrass edge and the drifting No. 11 silver and black floater appeared to become tangled in grass. The 10-pound test Trilene line held as he worked the fish to the boat without any problems.

The 28-inch long bass finally began her battle on a short line, but it was to no avail. The big female was put in the bottom of the boat to await (and unfortunately dry out and die) weigh-in some nine hours later. It measured 25 inches in girth and was just 2-1/2 pounds short of the state largemouth record. The angler thinks there are bigger ones in that lake and others nearby. The year prior, the lake produced a 13 pound, 5 ounce and a 12 pound bass in 30 minutes' time.

Likewise, Sunset Lake on the city's west side was relatively unknown until a mid-February bass catch which weighed 15 pounds,

Lake Conway and other Orlando waters are near to thousands of anglers but are often overlooked.

2 ounces. Neither fish was taken by anglers with sophisticated tackle or equipment. In fact, the latter was caught on a cane pole.

Another big fish lake is Lake Hart which, along with sister Lake Mary Jane, is located just east of highway 15 in southern Orange County. Lake Hart has been a long-time favorite of mine -- ever since the day I caught a ten pounder (and three other bass over five pounds) from its bulrush beds on the western shoreline. A week later, I came in second place in a relatively large bass tournament held on the two-lake chain.

Lake Hart is a beautiful 1,850 acre body of water that lies in the shadow of the popular East Lake Tohopekaliga. The perimeter rushes hold bass year around, but those on the west and south sides offer a little more depth and bigger fish. The canal by Moss Park and its stately oaks provide a shaded canopy to Lake Mary Jane. There, you'll usually find good numbers of largemouth in its abundant vegetation.

Mary Jane's 1,158 acres are surrounded by a beautiful pine forest. The bountiful grass patches on its western and northern shorelines yield largemouth in the spring and fall. This is a great lake for tossing your favorite spinnerbait.

Orlando's Fishing Pressure

Most of the fishing pressure on the city lakes are from occasional anglers. Seldom do the avid bass chasers put their rigs in the smaller lakes. Small boats are often the ticket to a nice bass in the Orlando area, since many of the waters do not have adequate launching facilities for the large bass rigs.

Lake Conway boat ramps can handle most trailerable craft, as can some of the larger waters in the city. Lake Holden, Underhill, Ivanhoe, and Clear Lake are popular boating and fishing waters. I saw two bass over 13 pounds taken from the latter lake in the late 1960s when I lived on its shore. Fish like those still swim there relatively unmolested.

Some of the other lakes in the Orlando area that are capable of yielding bass of giant proportions are: Gatlin, Jessamine, Catherine, Turkey, Highland, Porter, Johns and Copeland. I once caught and released three bass over six pounds from the latter's pad fields. A rubber frog lure tricked them and two smaller bass in less than 30 minutes from the lake that sits on the city's busiest street, Orange Avenue.

Those waters are not unique, however. Such action can be found in almost every one of the Orlando's waterways. In Winter Park and Maitland, a chain of seven lakes offer some exciting bass action. Water skiers are the most common users of the Winter Park Chain of lakes, and both canoers and pleasure boaters ply the shorelines, but the largemouth don't seem to mind.

Lake Virginia, the chain's southernmost body, is a busy 233-acres with a public ramp on its shores. Numerous bass are caught along its eastern perimeter. A launch ramp on 451-acre Lake Maitland also provides access. There's plenty of water and habitat to fish on the lake ... early on weekday mornings. Lake Mizell is one of the better largemouth waters on the chain, as is the 157-acre Lake Osceola.

If you can block out traffic noises and, in some cases, barking dogs on the shore, and concentrate on the bass, you'll be amply rewarded. Sometimes, however, even the waterways crowded with homes, businesses or condominiums are peaceful and quiet. The only noises are those of your topwater plug being sucked under.

As cars zoom past some of the most productive waters in Florida on their way to the world-famous mousetrap and whale-jump, activity beneath the waters goes on almost unnoticed. Only an occasional angler interrupts the lifestyle of Orlando's healthy bass population.

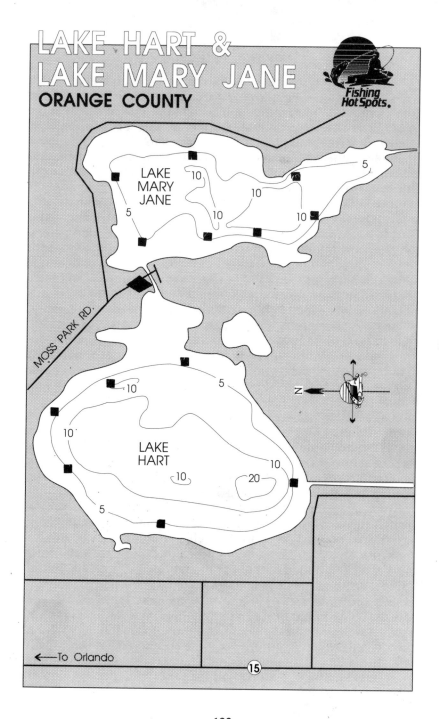

LAKE HART & LAKE MARY JANE
ORANGE COUNTY

Fishing Hot Spots.

LAKE MARY JANE

5

10

10

10

5

10

10

MOSS PARK RD.

N

10

5

10

LAKE HART

10

10

20

5

←To Orlando

15

123

THE BUTLER'S CHAIN

I've had the pleasure to be on the pretty Butler Chain (also called Windemere Chain) over a dozen times in the past couple of years, and it is a winner. Bass can be found on most of the 10 lakes in the chain that is partially surrounded by nice homes and always loaded with grass and cypress trees. The chain, located southwest of Orlando, doesn't yield its bounty easily, however. The more avid angler can do very well on it during the week, but the inexperienced fisherman may have some difficulty.

Lake Blanche is one of the chain's top largemouth producers. It and Tibet, Chase, Sheen, Pocket, Louise, Isleworth and Little Fish Lakes are all tannin-stained from their cypress perimeters. I've normally found the stained waters on Sheen on the southern end of the chain to be easier to catch bass in than the clear-water lakes like Butler and Down. The cypress knees, lily pads and grass edges on the south shore and the irregular grass beds on the north side of the lake tend to hold bass.

In stained waters, you can use heavier line and fish closer to the grass habitat without spooking the bass. You can also find sunken brush piles and more efficiently fish the numerous docks on most of the lakes. Additionally, an angler can toss spinnerbaits, topwater plugs and jerkbaits in shallower waters if his presence is less detectable.

Lake Butler, at 1,665 acres, is the largest lake in the chain and the most pressure by anglers. Skiers and cruisers pressure most of them. The best areas to fish are the grass flats, Bird Island off the eastern side and Grassy Island on the southwestern side. Check out the 30-foot deep holes with the depth finders and work them by trolling or with Carolina-rigged worms for action.

Some monster bass have been lost in the chain, and a few have been landed. One reportedly over 18 pounds swims in these waters. Areas to try for a lunker include Pocket Lake's east-side grass line, Lake Blanche's 30-foot deep holes and grass beds off its southeast shore, the mouths of the canals leading into and out of Lake Louise and the deep holes in Lake Chase.

For sheer numbers of largemouth, try Lake Down's coves and bays and Waseon Bay off Lake Butler. Fish the deep holes in each highly-developed lake, and keep an eye out for schooling activity. Lake Tibet's western shoreline is a fun spot to take several small bass. Little Fish Lake averages only about eight feet, but it offers good grass beds with bass, just off the shoreline.

Mike Paule (left), his son and a friend hold up a 17 1/2 pound Lake Rose bass.

Also, check out the mouths of all canals and in the waterways themselves for topographical changes; that's where the bass will be. A few of the canals are shallow enough to pose navigation hazards during low water, so be careful when moving through them. Try the chain on weekdays if possible to escape the boating pressure. If fishing on a weekend, pick the smaller lakes where skiing is less likely to interfere with your casting.

TAMPA'S TARPON TIME

Picturesque Lake Tarpon, about 20 miles north of Tampa and Clearwater, may be one of the best spring bass lakes in the state. A recent survey by the Florida Game and Fresh Water Fish Commission revealed that the catch rate of largemouth is about four times better than the state average.

"One of the reasons bass fishing is so good is because most bass caught are voluntarily released and not killed," explained Fishery Biologist, Tom Champeau. "Fishermen released 83 percent of the bass they caught, and that voluntary catch and release philosophy is quite unusual. On urban lakes, though, the greatest thing any angler can do to ensure a quality fishery is to release his catch."

Bass angler success was about one bass caught for every two hours of fishing, according to the information collected. The survey also revealed that bass fishing accounted for over 78 percent of the total angling effort on the lake named after a saltwater fish. A comparison of current fish population levels with similar data collected during the 1960's and 70's shows fish production has increased over the past decade.

The 2,534-acre Lake Tarpon off highway 19 in Pinellas County is the home of the officially documented state record largemouth, one that weighed 19 pounds even. It was caught on a live eel in 1961 (The unofficially-documented state record caught just north in Pasco County on Big Fish Lake in 1923 weighed 20 pounds, 2 ounces). Another giant an ounce less than 19 pounds was taken from Lake Tarpon that same year. The great big bass fishing of the 1950s was diminished somewhat by salt water intrusion prior to the construction of a dam, but the lake has come back and big catches of bass are very possible. One 16 pound largemouth was taken a few years ago.

The numerous docks, piers, fish attractors, an abandoned pipeline and other natural structure make these shallow waters productive. The lake only averages eight to 10 feet in depth, but it has a few deep holes down to 25 feet and about 15 miles of productive shoreline. Some of the better spots to try lie in the North Cove area, the east shore grass and cattail lines from Piney Point northward, and the grass edges from Dolly Bay to Salmon Bay on the west side of the lake. Fish the pilings, piers and holes in these areas.

Don't pass up the canals, especially those in Dolly Bay and Little Dolly Bay during the spring months. Other hotspots on Tarpon are the mouth of Otter Creek, Brooker Creek and Sandy Point, all on the eastern shore. Throughout the year, most of the hydrilla patches hold largemouth. Work the offshore vegetation in the summer and winter, and in the spring and fall, cast the shallower hydrilla. Also try the riprap and bridge pilings in the outfall canal. There are three launch ramps on this popular lake.

WADING THE ALAFIA

The Alafia River southeast of Tampa is a small, meandering stream that has its share of neglected bass. The bottom-scraping riffles along the 50-mile-long river keep the boat traffic limited to canoes and an occasional johnboat, but fishing pressure is nil. Wade fishermen like such opportunities.

This 15 pound, 2 ounce largemouth from tiny Sunset Lake was caught on a canepole.

The bass usually aren't large, up to two or three pounds at best, but the tranquility offered to anglers who wade its productive pools is unsurpassed. Numerous shallow points found along the Alafia most of the year discourage boat traffic and fishing pressure.

A few years back, I discovered wade fishing for bass was overlooked in this river. I caught and released about 15 little bass on my first trip down the Alafia. Stopping at each tranquil pool, I hopped out of my canoe and waded into the cool, refreshing waters. With air temperatures of 90 to 95 degrees and a limited water flow, the conditions were right for the bass to be in the four to six-foot-deep pools on the bends and beneath the riffles.

Bass were where I expected to find them, holding on structure in shallow water near deep-water protection. I was careful to approach them quietly, though, because shallow water bass spook easily. Where waters ran deeper, I was able to cast from the shallow points to most deep water bass haunts. The largemouth were lying in the quieter stretches, avoiding the moderate current near the middle of the tiny stream.

When walking along the Alafia, the wader should move slowly and not shuffle his feet. Silt and sand is usually picked up by moving water and can tip off the angler's presence to downstream inhabitants. That would void the advantage that a wader has over the bank-bound fisherman, that of being able to cast to spots regardless of overhanging trees along the shore.

I prefer to use small spinnerbaits, plastic worms and grubs when wade fishing. These single-hook lures provide a degree of safety when battling a feisty bass up close. More than once, I've had a powerful largemouth swim between my legs with a bait carrying treble hooks.

127

To get your share of bass on the Alafia, you have to be an accurate caster. It is essential. When wade fishing, you can generally control casts better and work closer to cover than can a boat fisherman. Short and accurate casts minimize hangups and produce more bass. It's easier to set the hook with a short, taut line.

Hillsborough Habitat

The Hillsborough River is 54 miles in length and drops 80 feet in elevation while draining 690 square miles. The river was first named "Mocoso," then "San Julian de Arriaga" by a Spanish explorer and later "Hillsborough" (after the Earl of Hillsborough) by the British. It supplies about 75 percent of Tampa's drinking water, in addition to providing recreation for many.

Around Tampa, several storm and sewage pipes empty into the black water river and bulkhead walls prohibit good bass habitat growth. Upstream of the dam, which impedes the natural flow, bass fishing can be good. The wilderness of the upper Hillsborough to the northeast offers cypress hammocks and sweet gum tree shorelines. The major tributaries are Blackwater Creek, Flint Creek, New River, Trout Creek and Cypress Creek.

The spring-fed river rises from the Green Swamp and is a lazy, meandering stream for several miles. Crystal Springs, a private recreation area, helps maintain the water level of the upper river. It is this region where bass anglers and canoers can both find happiness.

The Southwest Florida Water Management District owns 17 miles of riverfront on both banks, and the state owns another 3,000 acres of land at Hillsborough River State Park on highway 301. There are small, cascading rapids over a limestone outcropping at the park. Below that is an area called 17 Runs, and this section is only navigable by canoe.

The reddish-brown waters widen near Flint Creek, and from there on down, you can generally navigate with a motor boat. At Interstate Highway 75, a concrete flood-control structure hunches. The river banks from the structure downriver through a stretch called the Narrows and on to Fletcher Avenue are still fishable, and they do yield bass.

Bass fishing on the Hillsborough down to Lettuce Lake Park is often good in the spring when water levels are minimal and confined to its main channel. The Tampa Reservoir dam at 30th Street holds back the freshwater and ends the bass opportunities.

128

Lake Hart, south of Orlando, is a great fishing lake that lies in the shadow of larger "name" lakes.

Other waters near Tampa that offer some bass fishing include the upper portions of the 38-mile-long Little Manatee River in Hillsborough County, the 34-mile-long Anclote River (north branch) and the 41-mile-long Pithlachascotee River (nicknamed Cotee River) both in Pasco County, and Pleasant Grove Reservoir, a 647-acre Pleasant Grove Reservoir (officially named Ed Medard Reservoir) in southern Hillsborough County.

Lake Thonotosassa (819 acres) in Hillsborough County, tiny Lake Moon (99 clear-water acres) in Pasco County and Lakes Seminole (716 acres) and Alligator (72 acres) in Pinellas County are all overlooked Tampa area largemouth bass waters. Seminole also offers sunshine bass. All have public access.

13

NATIONAL FOREST ACTION

TUCKED INTO THE center of the 366,000-acre Ocala National Forest are more than 500 small waters that offer anglers unique largemouth bass habitats. Lesser-known waters, like Delancy, Kerr, Half Moon Lake, Lake Bryant and Mill Dam Lake, are accessible and productive, but they receive very little fishing pressure. Those waters are located near the town of Lynn, and fishing there and on other forest waters can be outstanding.

Trophy bass, like the one a guide friend caught a few years ago are regularly encountered in Half Moon Lake. A westerly 12 mph wind pushed Dan Thurmond's boat across the southern-most flats of the lake. Huge shiners swam behind four outfits. The baits had already fooled three bass in the previous two hours, including a six pounder.

Half Moon Lake and others in the forest have surprises waiting for bass fishermen.

Depths of 10 to 15 feet lay near the grass island where Thurmond and a friend began another drift. One hundred yards into the drift, a bobber slowly descended. It had, they thought, probably become entangled in isolated grass growing up from the lake bed. They soon realized that there was a fish on the line and the friend reared back on the seven-foot, heavy action rod to set the hook.

The huge bass reacted on her own terms and almost pulled the lightweight angler over the gunwale. As his friend struggled with the fish, Dan stumbled over rods and tackle boxes to grab a net. Dan's second attempt to net the largemouth was successful, and the bass was immediately hung on their scales. It pulled the needle to 11 pounds, five ounces, not bad for an often overlooked pothole in the middle of the forest.

Half Moon Lake, one of the largest and most productive waters in the forest, is 340 acres of relatively open water that's surrounded by 1,000 acres of 'wet' prairie. During normal water conditions, the prairie has one to three feet of water over most of it. The prairie grasses act as a filter to remove impurities and sediment from the water. Some holes dropping to eight or 10 feet may be present for the adventurous explorer with shallow-draft boat.

Sawgrass is abundant throughout the prairie section and is for the most part, impenetrable. Boat trails do exist in a few areas, most notably form the main body of Half Moon through the prairie to the 50-acre Bear Hole and to 20 acres of open water just off State Road 40. Launch ramps can be found near the Forest Restaurant on 40 and at the end of road "79D", which is reached by taking Forest Road 79 south from State Road 40 for about 2 miles.

Half Moon Lake, between Astor and Ocala off State Highway 40, is not well known among bass fishing addicts, but it does produce lots of big bass. Three largemouth over 13 pounds were taken from the small lake in one year. During one single week, seven fish over 11 pounds were caught from the main body of water whose name is derived from its shape. While the lake record is supposedly over 17 pounds, two largemouth over 16 pounds were taken about ten years ago by shiner-fishing anglers.

The lake has been very good to Thurmond and his guide clients. On one windy, clear day, they caught 13 bass on their large, wild shiners. Two were twins, weighing over eight pounds each. The anglers caught bass on every drift. The two biggest bass came during the mid-day period, which Dan feels is the best time to catch lunkers there. Nine out of ten of his big bass have been caught around noon.

Gator Holes In The Grass

Half Moon is a lake that I really enjoy fishing. Bass are usually willing to bite, and it is an excellent warm weather lake because of natural 'holes' almost 25 feet deep. Under normal water conditions, the average depth is close to 15 feet in the lake's main body. The prairie 'holes' should not be overlooked by visiting anglers with hopes of huge largemouth over 13 pounds. At least 10 major 'holes' exist in the prairies circling Half Moon and all have big bass in them.

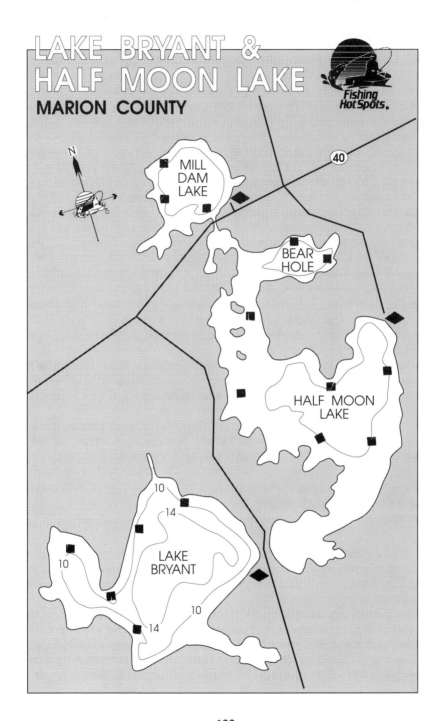

LAKE BRYANT &
HALF MOON LAKE
MARION COUNTY

Fishing Hot Spots.

N

40

MILL DAM LAKE

BEAR HOLE

HALF MOON LAKE

10
14
LAKE BRYANT
10
10
14

Most of the giant Half Moon bass have been taken from the open water 'holes' that were burrowed by alligators. Since early days, huge gators have enlarged and deepened the shallow flats. The constant traffic has kept down growth of the grass patches in several areas, making for slightly deeper water and the formation of small coves. The lake's `irregular' shoreline is also from apparent alligator movement and largemouth love the customized terrain.

Several gators exist in the swampy prairie around Half Moon, but they pose little consequence to bass anglers. While alligators on the main lake are scarce, the benefits from their earlier presence remains. During normal water levels, the prairie holes are accessible via boat trails to the main lake body. When drought conditions are present, the boat trails are useless.

The prairie holes are normally inaccessible to all, except those with 4-wheel drive swamp buggies. The main body of the lake has very few houses on its shoreline and the area around most prairie 'holes' is even more remote. In fact, most of the cabins and houses that exist on the lake are located on one prairie 'hole' adjacent to Highway 40. Many of the holes are so remote they have not been fished in the past few years.

Launching on the lake's main body or on the Bear Hole during extremely dry years is usually only possible with 4-wheel drive vehicles. Experienced anglers use an old roadbed that's adjacent to deep water shoreline off which to launch their bass boat.

Depths off Half Moon's east shoreline where the ramp is located appear to drop the quickest. Waters in the flats on the main body vary from eight to 14 feet with grass covered bottom. At normal levels, the deep waters are stained with a visibility of about three feet. Maximum depths approach 24 feet and several moderate drops occur throughout the lake.

TACTICS, LURES & BAIT

The flats are ideal areas for drifting live bait and so are waters along the westerly and southerly weed lines. Drifting the baits behind bobbers are generally preferred unless the sun is high and the lake is calm.

Area guides usually employ fluorescent orange corks for ease of visibility, and under normal circumstances, the vivid colors don't scare fish off. On bright days, however, the guides may put away the corks altogether and tight-line the shiners. They'll drift the baits in specific patterns, employing four rigs to maximize the coverage.

The small lakes in the Ocala National Forest are usually ideal spots for small boats and fun fishing.

Hooking the bait must be precise to prevent entanglements. Shiners are hooked through either the right nostril or left nostril for the outer rigs and through the lips and out between the nostrils for those rigs positioned mid-boat. This normally keeps the shiner rigs apart.

Bonnets are abundant on Half Moon, and they offer excellent largemouth habitat. In some of the better spots, the pad beds are still under water. The pad fields aren't quick to adjust to water level changes. Half Moon's southwest bank has an abundance of the bonnets which provide a line for drifting. Most anglers that work the area manage to catch several fish there. Big bass not in the main body of the lake are usually in the flooded prairies.

Schools of shad often surface on the lake, according to waterfront resident Ken Daubert. Bass surround and concentrate the shad. Then, the bass slash and cripple the shad until they scatter. Anglers tossing vibrating plugs, crankbaits and flashy topwater plugs with spinners often connect on a surface school. The baits are cast to the melee or just ahead of it.

Even after the main school of bass submerges, a few remain to cruise the surface and inhale crippled shad or chase down a straggler. The whole thing can last three or four very long minutes. If you are alert and work very efficiently, from the first panic of the shad through the blitz and until the last cripple is gulped down, you can catch several bass before they sound.

"In a minute or two, they'll be up again giving you another chance," he says. "Sometimes you can position yourself between several schools and work one while the other is down. The action can be exhausting, and at other times, it can be frustrating if you do not have the right lure."

"Sometimes, a fly may be needed," Daubert says. "I have watched conventional lure fishermen strike out in the middle of this type of schooling activity. They'll rake the boiling bass and shad with usually productive crankbaits and come up empty."

OTHER FOREST LAKE SCHOOLERS

Some of the other forest lakes that may offer good bassin' are Farles Prairie-Sellers Lake, a chain of lakes that have widely fluctuating water levels, Fore Lake, Mill Dam, Lake Delancy and Bryant. Ramps exist on most of the waters over 300 acres. There are 20,000 acres of ponds and lakes in the forest, so plenty of opportunity exists to capture schooling bass.

"You can easily catch 30 or 40 largemouth bass per morning or evening on many National Forest waters," says Daubert. "You can catch schooling stripers and sunshine bass in some lakes."

In the Ocala National Forest area, the prey species which trigger feeding behavior are the brook silverside, gizzard shad and threadfin shad. Brook silversides, according to the former fisheries biologist, are common in the maidencane borders of the lakes, and bass use teamwork to flush them out into open water. More largemouth will be waiting there too for the easy targets.

"When the bass are herding silversides, they tend to be very selective and lures must imitate the natural bait size, color and action," he explains. "Since these forage fish are most common in the gin-clear waters of the forest lakes, the bass get a very good

The variety of bass habitat from grass pastures, to floating bog "islands," to acres of pad fields all contain bass.

look at them. You can often spot them skipping over the water, one skip ahead of the bass' gulp."

Silversides are slim fish, from one to three inches long, pearl on the bottom, translucent green on the back, and they have a silver metallic stripe down the side. Chasing down these active but apparently very tasty baitfish is often a job for younger bass, and the average size caught tends to run small. Three pounders, though, are common enough to make them a good secondary target while you are waiting for bass to begin busting the schools of shad, according to Daubert.

Shad, a high-energy food for bass, are common in most of the larger lakes and rivers of the Ocala National Forest area. Threadfin shad can range up to eight inches in length, while gizzard shad can attain 18 inches. Most feeding bass that are encountered, though, will be thrashing the one- to four-inch long threadfin. The predators normally weigh one to four pounds; two to three pounders are most prevalent.

Lake Delancy yields numerous big bass in the winter and spring months. In fact, the lake yielded three bass over 14 pounds one spring and has a lake record of 16 1/2 pounds. The 382-acre clear waters offer a variety of cover and bottom topography to about 14 feet for interested anglers. The west side of the lake is a vast grass flat with waters that average five feet in depth. Its southern shoreline offers the deepest gator hole in the lake, a 24-footer.

The eastern side is like a conventional, saucer-shaped Florida lake and contains some 10-foot deep, open water areas with ridges and dropoffs along the bottom. This lake is perhaps the cleanest named lake in the forest. It can be reached off Forest Road 75 west of highway 19.

Lunkers in the Ocala National Forest lakes are most active in the spring as are most big bass on Florida waters. But, many guides catch bass over eight pounds year-round in the forest and wonder why more people don't fish for lunkers in the summer and fall. They are still there, waiting to be fed live bait or artificials.

Bass in The Forest Depths

In deep, relatively clear, open water lakes in the forest, suspended bass will rise further and stay up longer. They are often unusually large schools of bass, sometimes a hundred or more per school. There are sometimes many of these schools feeding at the same time when conditions are right.

Lake Bryant, which connects to Half Moon via culverts, has a unique schooling situation, according to Daubert. The water color is dingier and shallower on Bryant where the schooling activity takes place. In Half Moon, the fish usually school in 10 to 20 foot of water, but Bryant's bass often attack the shad in six foot depths over the sparse eel grass bottom.

The depths on the 767-acre lake that lies about 11 miles east of Silver Springs, range from about six to 14 feet with a few holes exceeding 20 feet. There are two marked fish attractors on the Marion County lake: one off the east shore, and the other in the southwest corner. Both are in 10 to 13 feet of water.

"The bass and the shad in Lake Bryant average larger than Half Moon, but there are usually less bass per school," he says. "They are less organized, and more unpredictable. However, they are much less selective due to the dingier water color. Any lure of roughly the right size will be taken when the bass are competing for the shad."

When I first visited Bryant in the early 1970s, the fish camp owner told me that the lake record was almost 18 pounds. I haven't heard of any larger since, but bass over schooler size are obviously

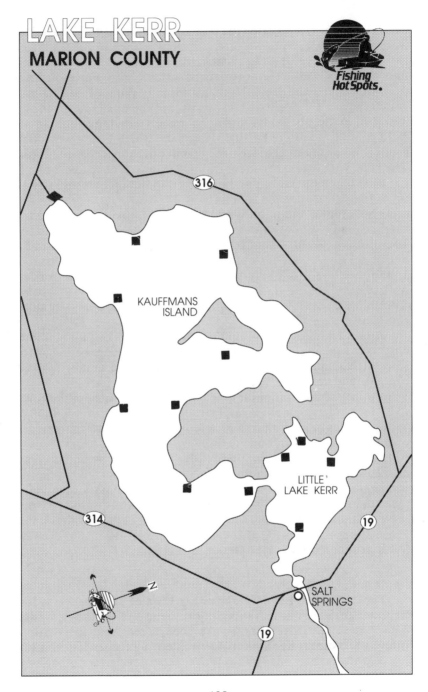

LAKE KERR
MARION COUNTY

Fishing
Hot Spots.

316

KAUFFMANS
ISLAND

LITTLE
LAKE KERR

314

19

N

SALT
SPRINGS

19

available here. Locals catch the big ones off the southern shoreline, west of the fish camp.

There are several other small forest waters that are overlooked bass hotspots. Good fishing exists on Sellers Lake, Farles Prairie, Chain-O-Lakes and Buck Lake, all just off Forest Road 95 and state highway 19. They also lie just east of the bombing range and are most enjoyably fished when jets are not buzzing overhead.

Sellers is a very clear 1,000-acre lake which is connected via small canals or boat lanes to other small ponds in a chain of lakes. The lake, with extensive underground springs, is deep and cool. It has excellent bass fishing, and a good ramp lies just off highway 19 on the northeast corner of Sellers.

The launch ramp to Buck Lake near the Forest Service campground is a poor one and accessible primarily to small boats. The dishpan lake is tannic acid stained with numerous pads and a perimeter of grass. The depth ranges to about 20 feet and the fish activity can be good. The lake also has about 3,000 acres of flooded prairie surrounding it, and that allows a perpetual forage base. Buck Lake is ideal for night fishing, where live bait is usually more productive than artificials.

Farles Prairie, like most of the other prairie lakes, is a shallow, clear lake that has large expanses of flooded maidencane and water lilies with deeper spots consisting of potholes and ponds. It has a campground and launch ramp at its south end off Forest Road 95. With weedy shores, alligator holes and some pothole depths down to 20 feet, it has numerous largemouth. Juniper Prairie is similar with potholes of from one to 20 acres scattered about sandy ridges of marsh. Clear waters and the thin depths make this lake very easy to wade, but do so with stealth in order to catch its bass. This lake also has an excellent camping area.

Beakman Lake lies near Sellers also and offers a nice quiet place to catch bass. Fishing the clear waters is well-protected from the winds. Two islands and a very irregular shoreline maximize the fishing opportunities. Mill Dam is a very clear little lake with few holes deeper than 10 or 12 feet.

Lake Kerr

The 2,830-acre Lake Kerr near the town of Salt Springs is the largest lake in the Ocala National Forest and one of the better bass holes. Bass up to 16 pounds have been taken from the shallow sloughs and canals by shiner fisherman during the spring months.

One man boats are ideal for the remote lakes in the Ocala National Forest. Fishing pressure is minimal in most.

Water depths of 15 feet or more and great clarity make tough conditions for those tossing artificials in the other months. Plenty of largemouth are present in the spring-fed lake, but they are easily spooked in the clear waters. Gradual slopes from the shallows and little bottom variation make this lake even more difficult to amass big catches of bass.

Some successful winter and summer anglers fish the spring holes on the lake floor, if they can find them, and others take to the water at night. The latter is common on waters with such visibility, and while it's not highly popular on Kerr, those who do fish by the moonlight don't always brag about their catches. They tend to keep such information "private."

Kaufman Island lies on the north side of the lake and really divides the lake into two sections: Lake Kerr and Little Lake Kerr. Summer anglers stick to the big lake while the little lake, also called Lake Warner in some documents, attracts fishermen in the fall and spring.

Small, deep-running crankbaits that resemble forage fish and bottom bumping plastic lures are most effective here. Successful anglers will also toss spinnerbaits around the grass, lily pads and isolated docks in the shallow, vegetated shallows, if possible.

FOREST BASICS

There are numerous nameless ponds deep in the forest that offer great bass fishing. Those with names may have a crude dirt ramp or launching area, while others may only take a canoe, johnboat or wade-fishing tube. Some you even have to hike into. If backpacking, camping and fishing are your thing, the 66-mile long Ocala Trail takes you close to 60 ponds and lakes. Some of the better, named ponds are Brooks Pond and Twin Ponds.

Lakes Charles, Eaton, Jumper and Lou are located north of Lakes Bryant and Half Moon and highway 40. Lou is 130 acres, and the others are just over 300 acres. These Marion County waters are dark, tannin-stained, but they do yield some big bass, particularly to shiner fishermen. The four lakes range in depth from only 4 to 10 feet. Fish the edges of the grass and pads on these lakes for action. On Charles, the abundant cypress knees often hold bass in the spring.

The 213-acre Grasshopper Lake and the 232-acre Wildcat Lake, both in Lake County, are other good bass lakes in the Forest, or as some affectionately call it, the "Big Scrub."

Many of the smaller ponds in the forest have only a rough sand road leading to them, making 4-wheel drive important to the adventuress. Those going down the back roads and paths should carry a CB radio (or cellular phone), a compass, a map and a good pair of binoculars, such as the 7 X 42 Jason Perma Focus floating model.

Topo maps showing the area in detail are available from the nearest U.S. Geological Survey office. A good map showing the Ocala National Forest, some of the roads and its lakes, can be obtained from Forest Supervisor, U.S. Forest Service, P.O. Box 13549, Tallahassee, FL 32308. There is a charge for the map.

For those who haven't fished the prairie waters of the Ocala National Forest, I would highly recommend it. There are many unique areas there with plenty of big bass. For those wanting to go it on their own, hook up a boat to the 4-wheel drive and go exploring!

SPRING RUNS BY DAY AND NIGHT

TINY HOMOSASSA RIVER north of Tampa is not a major player in the largemouth bass fishing game. It is just six miles long, and the spring-fed waters are relatively shallow and very clear -- tough conditions for the average Florida basser with 17 to 20 pound test. There are, however, plenty of bass to be caught, particularly at night.

As the summer begins to heat up, so does the nocturnal activity on the Homosassa, as a couple of Ohio gentlemen found out a few years ago. After a long, hard day of casting and little to show for their efforts, they decided to continue their fishing after sunset. The two reasoned that the better fishing just a couple of days before the full moon could be taking place at night.

The scenic streams of West Central Florida usually provide a great bass fishing experience.

As darkness settled in, they began casting Texas-rigged plastic worms around the numerous boat docks scattered along the west bank of the river. The tide had just turned and was incoming when they had their first strike. Five minutes later, they had three bass in the boat's livewell, and after an hour, they counted a limit each. They began to release bass and continued to fish.

They enjoyed catching a concentration of largemouth that few have ever experienced along one three-quarter-mile stretch between MacRae's Bait House and the north end of St. Catherine's Bay. Their best ten fish from that area averaged four pounds. They caught and released 75 bass that night and actually tired of catching bass. They again fished the day-tough river the following two nights and continued to find maximum activity on the river bass.

The Homosassa begins at the springs that bear the same name in Citrus County and dumps its crystal-clear waters into the Gulf of Mexico. The river, located just west of U.S. Highway 19 along County Road 490, is not noted as a trophy bass fishery, but it has yielded largemouth over 15 pounds. Night anglers have discovered some excellent fishing for what I call "mid-size" bass, those between five and eight pounds.

Early summer action, like that found on the Homosassa, occurs on many clear rivers around the state then. Most have exciting nighttime bass action awaiting anglers who fish with the moon rays in the sky when floating down a dark, tree-canopied stream.

Moonlit nights are an ideal time to be on the clear waters of a spring run. Bass under a "microscope" all day seem to lose their inhibitions after the sun sets. Those that spook at the approach of a small boat or the landing of a tiny rubber lure will aggressively charge a larger offering presented through the darkness. They probably strike harder and fight longer at night...or at least it seems that way.

With some source of light (the moon), an angler can easily navigate most spring runs. Most flow from point A to point B with very few islands or split channels along the way, so it is very difficult to get lost. About the only problem you'll encounter on a moonlit spring run is suffering from lack of sleep; hopefully, the bass will keep you up all night.

Most spring runs yield water at a fairly constant 72 degrees, so summer temperatures extremes are not a great factor in the bass activity. For anglers who disdain the heat at high noon, nightfall offers cooler temperatures. If it's still too hot, one can always dip a foot overboard into the cool spring water. One caveat to note, however, is that the alligators do much of their prospecting at night, so be careful when dangling a foot beside the boat.

Oklawaha Charm

It was one of those brutally hot days when I took my first night float down the Oklawaha River. The thermometer said 95 degrees and the humidity was reading higher as my partner and I drove to launch our boat at the little park alongside S.R. 40 east of Ocala and Silver Springs. The river is clearer from there downstream due to the effects of the Silver River tributary and numerous other springs.

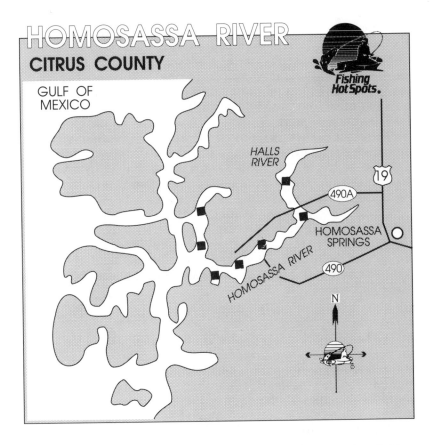

The Silver River and, for sheer boating pleasure (no fishing allowed) Silver Springs, near Ocala, are pretty day-time spots to visit. The narrow clear stream flowing from the Springs has an impenetrable jungle on both banks, including monkeys, descendants of those appearing in old Tarzan movies. Such natural discharges keep the effects of pollution minimal and the fishery healthy.

The normally skittish fish along the Oklawaha are often off-guard at night along that stretch of primitive wilderness. The current is swifter in that portion of the Oklawaha and the bordering forest more canopied, so the night float offers additional intrigue and excitement. The river is not particularly deep, averaging five to 10 feet in mid-channel, so shallow-running lures are productive.

I chose a spinnerbait, while my partner selected an in-line spinner. As darkness set in, his bait attracted the first of our 25 strikes that night, and a two-pounder was soon resting comfortably in the live well. My spinnerbait soon produced two smaller bass and his Snagless Sally accounted for one of about five pounds.

We had floated about a mile before we lost our first fish. It was one of several strikes that went awry during the course of the night. The single-hook lures that we chose were more weedless and safer to fish at night, but in the dense jungle that often surrounds the river, they can be more difficult for the bass to accurately strike.

The most exciting part of our float trip that night occurred after my partner had switched to a small topwater plug. A huge fish exploded on the lure as it hit down near some dark overhanging bushes. A solid hookup caused the giant fish to wallow on the surface as it began to pull line from the reel.

Obviously, we were hoping that it was a world-record largemouth, but the powerful fish fought differently. Big mudfish often do the same thing, but in the darkness, we couldn't identify the species before the 20-pound test monofilament gave way. Whatever kind of fish that was, it was a mean one and probably king of the Oklawaha.

Dark Wilderness Adventure

We enjoyed our float beneath the overhanging trees, and after our eyes adjusted to the darkness, we were able to easily see most of the cypress knees, willows, deadfalls, lily pads, arrowgrass and rock outcropping that hug the shoreline. While the bass commonly hug those structures during the day, they roam freer at night. Casts still have to be fairly accurate, though, to attract the normally suspicious largemouth.

We had plenty of fish that night to keep us awake. We switched to Texas-rigged plastic worms for a mile or so and caught several bass. Some anglers don't realize the effectiveness of such lures after dark. While the worm doesn't give off a thumping vibration or stir up the water on top, it does move along the bottom, emitting sound waves. Bass pick up on them easily in their crystal-clear environment. They have to have such keen senses to survive in a spring habitat.

The night bassin' is especially good all along the river from where Silver Spring's 500 million gallons per day enters. As on any vegetation-abundant spring run, a productive angler must use sharp hooks and tackle heavy enough to quickly pull the fish away from the numerous snags. The current is not too forgiving, so the opportunities come and just as quickly go. Successful fishermen are ready at all times.

Bass in clear water can be a challenge, particularly those larger specimens.

Anglers don't generally float the Oklawaha River in search of monster largemouth. They are after great numbers of bass. That's why I was mildly shocked when a giant bass suddenly overpowered my crankbait on another daytime trip down the river. The largemouth headed away from the brush-lined bank toward the center of the 50-foot-wide stream. It peeled line from a casting reel with tightened down drag for about 20 feet.

Then, the hooks straightened. I never even saw the bass, but it was perhaps the most powerful fish I have ever had on. Giant largemouth are fairly rare on the river, but they do show up occasionally. Anglers after the bass of their dreams usually head upstream to one of the Harris Chain of Lakes or to the Rodman impoundment. As a result, the bass in between are usually overlooked, and that includes those in the trophy class.

Floating down the tree-lined Oklawaha waterway casting to the shady pockets behind fallen timber is a great way to escape angling pressures found elsewhere in the state. With nearly 50 miles of twisting river and beautiful scenery, the Oklawaha certainly provides anglers plenty of bass opportunities. This portion of the Oklawaha has always been kept a secret by those knowledgeable anglers who love its charm.

GETTING ON AND ALONG THE RIVER

There are numerous access areas along the river for those wanting to try the bass-filled river. Since there are no fuel facilities or marinas on the water, that's good. The ramp at Highway 40 near Silver Springs is a good one. There are a couple of ramps at Eureka, one on either side of the bridge, and they are ideal for launching smaller craft.

Some ramps spread out along the river may be more suited for 4-wheel drive vehicles. A ramp at Paynes Landing on the west side of the river between the towns of Eureka and Orange Springs is very remote and difficult to find, but it allows a boat to launch in a section of the river with very little traffic. A good ramp is located at Orange Springs near the headwaters of Rodman. From there, anglers can boat upstream for several miles and float down.

The Moss Bluff locks have a 21-foot differential in water level which can be a 'trip' just going through. Below this one (and the Haines Creek lock) is superb fishing in the spring and fall. The constant pumping of water to raise or lower elevation levels is a catalyst for feeding bass.

The locks release huge amounts of water and, in the process, wounded baitfish. The park area at Moss Bluff provides excellent bank fishing, as well as a family picnic area and good boat ramps. Successful anglers fishing the lock spillway overflow area employ heavy weights on their worm rigs to reach the bass.

OTHER WEST COAST SPRINGS

Fishing any of Florida's 17 major spring runs anytime is seldom uneventful or dull. The same goes for another 49 smaller springs that spawn clear-water runs. In fact, 46 of the state's 67 counties have springs, so there are plenty of opportunities for such excitement. Many of the clear water streams are short, but that doesn't mean they are void of largemouth.

Crystal River in Citrus County is just seven miles long from its head springs, and the Chassahowitzka stretches only about five miles before pouring into the Gulf. Both, although fresh water for

With nearly 50 miles of twisting river and beautiful scenery, the Oklawaha certainly provides anglers plenty of bass opportunities.

the majority of their length, are tidal influenced, but the bass in each still grow big. Ten pounders have been taken from each, and that's not unusual productivity for a spring run, even a short one.

The clear Crystal River, which is derived from the second largest spring in the state, plus 29 other known springs in the headwaters area known as King's Bay, has a constant water temperature of 72 degrees. As a result, it usually produces the best fishing for small largemouth bass in the fall and winter each year. Many of the large springs here, such as King's Spring, Grand Canyon Spring and Mullet Spring, are primarily utilized by scuba divers and snorkelers.

The river has a manatee "watch," but few of the endangered creatures are obstacles during the summer months. Scuba diving and canoeing are sports that are participated in on this river. Civilization is very apparent on the twisting waterway; there are primitive areas, but the fishing can be best around the man-made boat docks, piers and bulkheads.

The six short, narrow tidal creeks that cut paths through the sawgrass off the river's northern shore can also yield largemouth on occasion, particularly on an outgoing tide. The waters there are clear and very shallow, and the fishing generally improves as you move upstream. Several small bays off the creeks harbor the bass which seldom grow over three pounds in this brackish water.

Lightweight plugs and small lures produce best creeks off Crystal River in the winter months, and some anglers in the know have caught and released over 30 largemouth at times.

A small boat and motor is better suited for moving about the Chassahowitzka, due to it being very shallow in spots. It is also surrounded by numerous overflow swamps which tend to "suck up" the baitfish and bass action when tides are high. Fishing is best on a falling tide when the bass have abandoned the bordering marsh areas. Little exists in the way of landmarks on the tiny river since the banks are part of the Chassahowitzka National Wildlife Refuge.

In the Chassahowitzka, flippin' plastic worms along the bulrush-lined banks is often productive. Small jerkbaits and "slug-type" soft plastics also fool largemouth. Topwater plugs, like Griffin's "Jerkin' Sam," are effective early and late in the day and during the spring and fall months.

The 5-1/2 mile long Rainbow River is where I've photographed numerous bass underwater for my articles and books. The beautiful waters that dip to between 10 and 20 feet in some places around the springs are crystal clear, so fishing is tough. Fish this Withlacoochee tributary in low light times for best results. As in the other spring-fed rivers, water temperatures range around 70 to 72 degrees. Fast retrieves with crankbaits and vibrating plugs are most productive in these waters.

In the winter, spring-fed waters are difficult to beat. The scenic streams of West Central Florida not only provide great bass fishing during the day or night, they usually offer an unforgettable experience.

15

EAST CENTRAL SPRINGS ACTION

MY FIRST EXPERIENCE on Salt Springs Run was only about one hour long; it was actually an extension to an afternoon on Lake George. We had caught only four bass in about five hours on the big lake when we discovered a concentration of largemouth at the mouth of the run. As the sun settled we started to catch bass, and when the strikes stopped after seven fish, we moved upstream to try the clearer waters. We floated maybe 3/4 of a mile of the run and caught another seven bass.

The bass action springs forth around Lake George and other Central Florida rivers.

Salt Springs Run, located 30 miles northeast of Ocala on Highway 19, is one of three spring runs that feeds into Lake George and offers excellent bass fishing. Salt Springs Run dumps over two million gallons of clear water each hour into the lake, five and one-half miles away. The canopy of sweetgum, cypress and pine and profuse shoreline vegetation along the primitive Ocala National Forest waterway makes for some interesting angling. The clinging weed growth actually renders some lures difficult to fish in these waters.

Taylor Lake is one of several wide spots in the run that yields numerous bass over 20 inches in length. The sand-bottomed run downstream and up offers chunky largemouth of similar proportions. The series of "lakes" along the upper reaches of the run and deeper holes nearby have submerged vegetation which harbor the biggest of bass. There are few depths exceeding 10 feet.

The lower two miles of the run offer a narrow, well-defined route into Salt Cove on the big lake. Faster currents in this stretch, though, require consideration of navigation control. Casting accuracy is most important then as well. Access ramps near the spring head and a shallow sandbar near the run's mouth on Lake George make small boats most suitable for this run.

Nearby on the western shore of George in the Ocala National Forest is Silver Glen Springs Run which contributes over three million gallons of water every hour. That's 72 million gallons of 72-degree water daily. The gin-clear stream that wanders through the dense forest attracts large crowds of boaters on the weekend, but if you can fish the run during the week, you may catch several bass. During the spring spawning season, you may catch some giant largemouth from the thick grass beds that are interspersed with white sand bottoms.

The tiny, one mile long run is one of the prettiest spring beds in the state. Silver Glen, located five miles north of the intersection of S.R. 40 and U.S. 19, has a boat ramp, or one can enter the run from George. Silver Glen Springs has a large marina with water, hookups, fuel and boat rentals. Anglers can usually float the small waterway three or four times in a short day. They'll catch bass, too.

The third Lake George spring run is called Juniper. The nine-mile wilderness trip down Juniper Run, offers beautiful tropical scenery and unique opportunities for largemouth bass of huge proportions in the spring months. The run is as small as 40 feet in width, and there are numerous shoals and ravine eddies along its twisting path. During the summer and fall, smaller bass can be fooled by anglers using a stealth-type approach to the river bends.

The picturesque Wekiva River, about 20 miles north of Orlando, feeds Lake George indirectly through the St. Johns River. Almost 50 million gallons of water gushes from the Wekiva daily, and it flows through semi-wild subtropical country, renown as a canoeing trail. The 16-mile-long waterway does abound in bass and is often overlooked by anglers. Small craft will find the 'jungle' cruise for largemouth very interesting.

For the first seven miles, the river varies from 15 to 300 feet in width as it passes numerous islands. Then, the Wekiva broadens to channels of slower currents for the next three miles. The final stretch is narrow with swift currents through an unspoiled canopy of cypress and hardwoods. Near the St. Johns, the beautiful river widens and slows once again.

The river swamps and uplands including its main tributary, the nine-mile-long Rock Springs Run, are owned by the State. The Little Wekiva River enters near Longwood, and all three waters

Fishing most spring runs is one way to escape the crowds and catch a bunch of largemouth. Smaller boats are perfect for many waters.

are designated as Outstanding Florida Waters, thus legally protecting their water quality from degradation. Good bassin' in the lower stretches of the rapidly flowing spring water near growth-oriented Orlando should be guaranteed.

Another tributary, Blackwater Creek, feeds into the river east of Orlando. It begins at Lake Norris and twists through a seemingly impenetrable jungle of trees and snags that make navigation feasible only by small boat during normal to high water conditions. The creek loses itself traversing a swamp in one section. There are bass in this navigational nightmare, however.

You can fish the lower end of the river by boating upstream from the Wekiva at a point about five miles above highway 46. There are actually two entrances, so you can choose either. Check out the beautiful little creek for some interesting small bass action.

FLOAT FISHING THE LIMESTONE SPRING BELT

Those four springs and many others around Central and North Florida are in what I call the "Limestone Spring Belt." Vast

153

deposits of limestone exist on surrounding land areas that were once covered by the ocean. In this region, deposits are very near the surface and both springs and sinkholes are numerous in many locations. Many springs are sources of large, navigable rivers, with mouths often 100 feet across. Thousands of lesser springs and sinkholes are also found in many river systems. More than 20 Florida springs in the region discharge at least 65 million gallons of water daily. The springs erupt from ground water through the lime deposits. As limestone is washed away, cavities are formed through the soil, resulting in the development of runs and sinkholes.

Sinkholes are formed as the water is 'sucked' into the earth. When surface water trickles down through a thin crust of lime to a cavity below, the structure weakens and a cave-in results. The underground water action, formed when a head of pressure builds and pushes water to the surface, gives birth to runs, such as Salt Springs, Juniper and Silver Glen. Float fishing one of the spring runs can be a beautiful and rewarding experience.

Spring-influenced rivers are often characterized by limestone banks, rocky shoals and strong currents. A canopy of moss-draped cypress, oak and maple is fairly common to the often narrow, twisting river banks. Shoals and shallows often limit boat traffic near the headwaters of tributaries. The downstream ends are usually navigable, however.

A pleasant float trip is usually possible on most watersheds. Spring upwellings through the limestone caverns in many of the waterways initiate substantial currents that can quickly sweep a boat downstream. Fishing the heavy currents is a unique challenge. The limestone shoals will play havoc on the tackle, and the angler will often have to crank up the outboard and motor back upstream to retrieve a snagged lure.

"One of the neatest trips I've taken was one to Alexander Springs Creek," friend Bing McClellan related. "The launch ramp off highway 52B is primarily for small boats and the waterway upstream is very pretty. There is plenty of grass and pads near shore with quiet pools four to six foot deep lying off the channel."

Bing used spoons and buzz baits to catch several largemouth from the pools which varied from 20 to 40 yards wide. He also used a plastic worm to fool some small bass, but the largest fell for a topwater plug. Largemouth of four and 5-1/2 pounds each sucked in the Rebel Pop-R and gave Bing a small spring creek thrill he won't soon forget.

154

Realistic-looking plugs are most effective in small clear water rivers and spring runs.

WHAT TO EXPECT

Most spring runs are clearest during low water. Rates of flow in the runs will vary with the fluctuating water table, as does the water level. Even in the stained river systems, the water is generally clear in the fall and winter. Algae during the summer rainy season will normally darken the water. Springs near the banks of surface rivers will also become very dark during periods of heavy rainfall.

In the East Central Florida region, most spring runs contain largemouth of up to 12 pounds, and many other springs yield particularly impressive specimens as well. The largemouth record for some exceeds 15 pounds, and bass weighing over 14 pounds have been caught from several rivers in the area. These rivers are well-known for their fishing opportunities, but they are just a few of the many waterways spawned from the spring/sinkhole network in Florida's limestone base.

The best time of the year to fish the river systems is during high water periods, due to the presence of bottom-scraping shoals in most. Late spring through October is a good time to find adequate water and plenty of bass. The rivers' temperature will remain fairly cool in mid-summer, providing day-long angling activity even when the afternoon sun bears down.

The underground network of waterways in the limestone spring region is complicated. The two dozen major spring-influenced rivers running across the surface are not. Fishing for bass in the high-visibility waters normally encountered in them can be relatively easy and successful.

As with any float trip, the entrance and exit locations should be planned in advance. Many anglers will embark at a downstream location, boat upstream to a selected spot and then drift back downstream a few miles to the convenient exit ramp. Most of the enjoyable fishing floats through the unspoiled spring runs take about an hour per mile.

Tactics, Lures & Bait

Discussing a 'typical' spring run may be misleading because seldom do they ever closely resemble each other. Successful bassin' techniques, however, tend to produce in all of them. Spring bass love crayfish, which composes a majority of their diet, so lures that resemble such morsels are usually effective. Most river bass will wallop artificials fished super slowly and near the bottom.

One favorite lure often used by locals is a jerkbait or injured minnow-type plug. Casts are timed to set the lure upstream of an overhanging structure, such as a limb or tree trunk. The lure is then allowed to drift into the bass-bearing cover. A twitch or two above the structure, and a submerged retrieve out of the cover once it reaches it, is effective.

Fallen and submerged trees and limbs are favorite spring bass haunts, and a Berkley Power Worm or Culprit Jerk Worm are popular lures. Rising water can trigger bass into feeding binges where they will tear up every pumpkinseed or moccasin-colored worm in the tackle box, but timing is important. Once the water level has inundated the tree-lined banks, bass are difficult to locate, hot bait or not.

The root system of fallen, shoreline trees along a spring run will many times appear partially above the surface. A deep shoreline with root structure aplenty appears often in the better stretches of a river. Root structures may be the only 'wet' part of the fallen tree. The tree will be blown down and fall on the bank, and then the current will erode away the dirt underneath the root structure, helping it to sink. Most of the trees along the various spring runs have four to five feet of water in front of them, and plenty of depth to hold bass.

Many of the spring runs have tree canopies and varieties of productive cover.

    Altering retrieves and changing lure sizes as conditions warrant is important for angling success. Heavy rains and high water generally mean less clarity, larger lures and slightly heavier line required. A noisier retrieve might be more productive under these conditions, as well.

    Low water means highly spring-influenced conditions and very clear waters. The bass become more spooky and more difficult to trick into striking floating minnow imitators then. Boat and lure control may be more difficult as new structure rises above the spring run's surface. Worm-fishing at that time may be more productive.

    Spring runs in the East Central part of the region offer unique experiences and lots of bass to those in the know. Newcomers, however, can often find a boat with a chipped or scratched hull and simply follow it!

16

BASS IN THE WILD WOODS

EVEN THOUGH LAKE Weir is one of the larger bodies of water in the state, it receives little attention from the hoards of bass fishermen in the state. That may be because the lake is not near a resort center, or even a large city; it lies between Wildwood and Belleview just east of Interstate Highway 75. There are very few facilities on it, and promotion is seldom valued by locals, who are quite happy to keep the bass activity secret.

Lake Weir has a "small bass" reputation among Central Florida bass chasers and is known for quantity catches. Twelve-pound bass and up are not taken regularly from these waters as they are on other lakes within an hour's drive from Weir. The lake has drinking water-type visibility and is difficult to fish for trophies. Lunkers are either buried in 14-foot-deep weed beds or in some of the drops that occur in the waters that average 27 feet deep and max out at around 35.

Lakes Weir and Panasoffkee just off the turnpike and interstate offer productive routes for bass.

But despite the lack of notoriety and facilities, Lake Weir may be one of the easiest waters in Florida to catch several largemouth in an early morning or late afternoon stretch. Several ramps strategically placed around the lake accommodate visiting boaters.

Fishing pressure on Weir is minimal, so it is possible to catch 10- to 14-inch bass fairly easily. While there are several tournaments a month on the lake, 20 or 30 boats can disappear easily on 5,685 acres. Some of the tournament activity takes place at night, when the lake's population feeds heavily on the prolific insect life and soft ray forage fish. A weekly contest at night during the summer attracts a dozen or more boats and the weigh-in prior to midnight often sports a six pound largemouth.

The clear water can pose problems to the anglers who tackle Weir with 30-pound test line. Heavy equipment does have its place after dark, though. I have usually been able to get away with 17 pound test line on overcast or windy days when the lake's surface is choppy and sunlight penetration into the depths is limited.

I've found that relatively light line is generally most appropriate in the deeper regions of Weir. Excessive weed growth or submerged brush is not a problem here. Rat-L-Traps produce in open water adjacent to the vegetation fields. Chrome Norman crankbaits on 12 and 14 pound test mono also take plenty of bass from the grass edges. Regardless of the tackle, the successful bass chasers on Weir take advantage of any low light situations.

The Light Show

Lake Weir has some interesting bass fishing that is seldom found on more remote waters. Largemouth move under the numerous boat docks and fishing piers that perforate the perimeter or into the deep weed beds that are abundant just off all shorelines. At night, the dock fishing gets even better.

Lights on the end of the dock start the food chain. Light penetration into Weir's crystal clear water attracts red minnows. A healthy influx of bugs around the lights are the siren. Tiny two-inch forage fish are drawn out of the darkness by the thousands of bugs to the six-feet of water under most docks. Red minnows form a swirling circle below glaring boat house lights, strategically placed just three feet from the water's surface.

Millions of baitfish churn in the water. The red minnows are 'running' on Lake Weir, and hungry bass are usually waiting to gorge themselves on the morsels. Massive schools of red minnows gather collectively each spring on the lake, and smart anglers rise early or stay out late to take advantage of the unique two to four-week long event.

A friend found the action to be unforgettable. He arrived at another friend's house at 5 a.m. and walked out on the dock to the boat house. The mass of minnows attracted to near-surface lights was circling, and in the dark, largemouth forms cruised beneath the swirling baitfish. Most of the shadows seen moving through the light rays were judged to be between about three pounds.

Preparation for the impending action began a day earlier when the two anglers seined several dozen minnows from the shallow

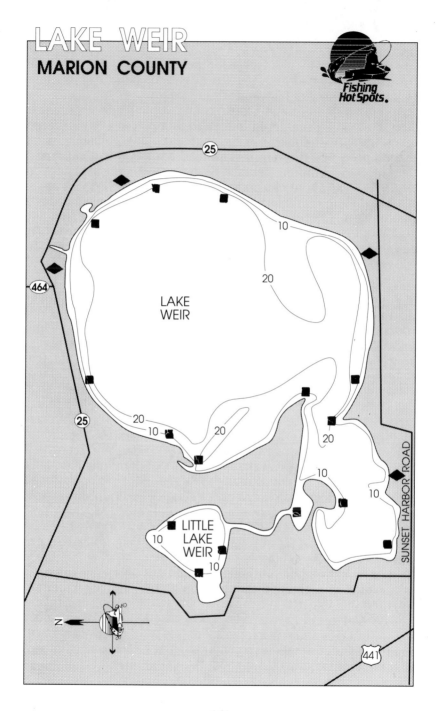

LAKE WEIR
MARION COUNTY

Fishing
Hot Spots.

25

10

20

LAKE
WEIR

464

20

25

20
10

20

20

10

10

10

LITTLE
LAKE
WEIR

10

10

SUNSET HARBOR ROAD

N

441

reeds on Weir's east shore. The bait-gathering took only an hour, and the men were amply stocked for the action. They dropped their baitfish into the midst of the swirling minnows and lowered them to a point about two feet beneath the mass.

Each man had an immediate strike from battling largemouth. They landed the bass, rebaited, and again placed their minnows below the baitfish concentration. A couple of two pounders struck the minnows and the action continued until they had amassed a limit in just 35 minutes. The 20 largemouth were typical Lake Weir size, averaging about two pounds apiece.

The unique approach to fishing for bass during the red minnow runs on the big body south of Ocala takes place in the darkness and dissolves with dawn. The first hour at dusk and the last one before dawn are the best times for this particular action. The minnow masses disperse when the sun shows up, and so do the bass.

WHERE TO LOOK

Lake Weir, and its small 400-acre sister, Little Lake Weir, are connected by a canal that averages from seven to 10 feet in depth under normal water conditions. Early rains in the year typically help the fishing. Although Florida droughts can deter fishing that canal, it can produce good bass action when low. During the spring, bass can be caught from the middle of that small canal.

Bass will generally be in deeper water on Weir due to the clarity, and plastic lizards rigged Texas-style will take their share of big ones. These bodies of water are deeper than many of Florida's natural lakes; even Little Lake Weir drops to just over 20 feet. While not a typical shallow 'dishpan' lake, Weir does have profuse aquatic vegetation in the form of peppergrass and maidencane. The clean sand bottom slopes downward slowly from shore. This is great largemouth habitat. Bass are taken year round by those pounding the shorelines with any lure that will climb through the weeds. Some anglers have caught and released up to 40 fish of up to six pounds on a spring day.

In summer weather, successful locals fish waters nine to 14 feet deep which have grass patches growing to the surface. Other hot weather spots to try are the two fish attractors placed by the Florida Game and Fresh Water Fish Commission in Weir's deep water. In Little Lake Weir, the drops just off the dense grassbeds to the left of the canal (as you enter the lake) often have produced summer bass for me.

Clear water Lake Weir is an excellent night fishing place where bass grow big.

There are a few other productive drops on Lake Weir where anglers familiar with structure fishing can apply their tricks. Lemon Point on the southwest side of the lake has a drop that quickly goes to 30 feet, and Bird Island has several 'holes' around it. Most of the larger bass are taken from such areas.

While no creeks exist in the Weir watershed, Red River on the north shore is a gully that provides runoff during the 'wet' season. Lunker bass are taken from the weed beds in this area. The lake record of 17 pounds, 3 ounces was taken several years back, but a couple of others topping 14 pounds give an indication of the potential in these waters.

The long stretches of grass fields are broken occasionally by beds of lily pads and pickerel weed on the south shore and by the boat houses on the north and east shoreline. Those docks hold lots of fish. They are particularly productive summer spots for largemouth hiding in the protective shade.

Tactics, Lures & Bait

Plastic worms 'flipped' under Weir's wooden docks account for great numbers of bass and fun activity. I've found that working each post supporting the dock will bring maximum action. The ends of the docks hold fish, even in the winter, and the adjacent weed bed points also give up an occasional lunker. Using six to eight-inch wild shiners can help put together an impressive tally.

To equip a lunker hunter with shiners, local guides often plant chum just below the docks. Dog food, bread cakes, hog pellets, etc., can be used to attract the attention of wild native shiners. When buying them, most accomplished live bait fishermen prefer the large river shiners. They are healthier and their scales are tougher due to constantly operating in a current.

Spinnerbaits worked through the heavy vegetation also do well year round. Largemouth work the shallows early and late during the summer months and take jerkbaits readily. Worms and deep running cranks are effective midday in the 12 to 14-foot depths below the weed lines. Most locals prefer weedless-rigged plastic worms in pumpkinseed, brown or red shad colors, and they employ a 3/8 or 1/2 ounce sliding bullet weight. Trolling deep running crankbaits through the depths is another productive summer ploy.

Fall bass chase topwater baits in thin water, while the plastic baits are productive in depths down to eight feet. During the frigid winter months, when the mercury often dips into the 30's or 40's, local anglers search the seven to 14 foot depths near maidencane. Plastic worms, spinnerbaits, and live shiners entice winter action.

Spring brings largemouth to shallower waters for spawning purposes. Weir bass tend to bed deeper, as much as 10 feet, due to the water clarity. Once the lovemaking duties are complete, the bass become aggressive again attacking crankbaits, worms and weedless spinners around the outer edges of the grass fields, or of course, red minnows beneath the spotlit docks after hours.

Lake Details & History

Lake Weir is not without development, but numerous lakefront homes and numerous summertime water skiers have not adversely affected the largemouth population. Half of the 38 miles of shoreline is dotted with houses and their boat docks, fishing piers

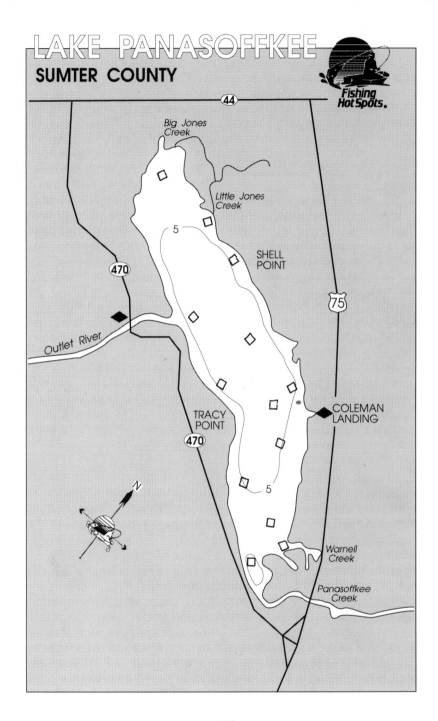

LAKE PANASOFFKEE

SUMTER COUNTY

44

Big Jones
Creek

Little Jones
Creek

5

SHELL
POINT

470

75

Outlet River

TRACY
POINT

470

COLEMAN
LANDING

5

N

Warnell
Creek

Panasoffkee
Creek

Fishing Hot Spots.

and swimming beaches. Several are even equipped with helicopter pads and at least one seaplane regularly lands each day. Weir is not a wilderness lake; there is activity of all kinds on it.

Waterfront residents are content to catch an occasional panfish from their pier, or just attend to their gardens. Other interests usually take priority over fishing. Probably the most renown lakeside residents were the infamous "Ma" Barker, her husband Fred and his mother "Machine Gun" Kate. The trio had established a hideout in a two story frame house on the north shore.

The sleepy hamlet of Oklawaha woke up one January morning in 1935 to the sounds of machine gun fire. The famous shootout between the FBI and the Barker gang took place at the very house that still stands. The agents had blocked off all the roads to town and had completely surrounded the house prior to the siege.

The Barker gang exchanged rounds of ammunition with the FBI who were stationed in the surrounding pine trees. Tear gas canisters were shot into the house, forcing the gang nearer the windows where they were easier targets. When the fighting was over that afternoon, the Barkers lay dead. The headlines are long gone, but the legend lives on.

For those wishing to try these Marion County waters, Weir can be reached off I-75 by taking the Belleview exit (Highway 484) just south of Ocala and going east on Alt. 27-441 for six miles. From Leesburg, travel 12 miles north on Highway 27-441 to the lake. A few overnight accommodations exist near the lake, but try Wildwood, Leesburg or Ocala for the best selection.

Panasoffkee's Big Bass

Sumter County's best bass fishing usually takes place in the 4,460-acre Lake Panasoffkee located a dozen miles or so south of Wildwood just off the interstate and highway 470. Contrary to the Seminole Indian meaning of "deep valley," the lake averages only about six feet and offers a few "deep" holes of 10 feet. Panasoffkee's 25 miles of shallow shoreline is weedy, extremely weedy, but the hydrilla and eelgrass cover makes it very "bassy."

The lake also has more than its share of other types of vegetation, such as peppergrass, bulrushes, cattails, lily pads, water hyacinths and sawgrass. The lake's clear waters and profuse vegetation make this lake tough fishing for some anglers, but certain tackle and methods help improve your odds. Most successful anglers fish offshore areas, away from the swampy shallows.

The Panassoffkee tributaries are covered with profuse vegetation, but persistent bass anglers can catch fish.

While some anglers struggle with the overly-abundant vegetation on the lake's gently-sloping southern, eastern and northern shores in search of their quarry, others have learned to fish the middle of the lake where a firm bottom and vegetation offers great success. One guide friend has caught three bass that all were just a few ounces shy of 14 pounds. Overall, he has caught and released close to 100 bass over 10 pounds in weight.

The "topographical" variations on this lake are in the form of submerged plant tops, not the bottom which is mostly shell, marl and muck. The six-mile long by one-mile wide lake is fed partially by the five creeks entering it; Panasoffkee Creek, Big and Little Jones Creek, Warnell Creek and Yellow Water Creek, and the corresponding regeneration areas adjacent to the tributaries. The underground aquifer, though, is probably responsible for feeding the lake with more water than all the creeks combined.

Little Jones Creek on the northern shore is one of the better areas on these waters, according to my guide friend. It has yielded impressive catches over the years to plenty of visiting anglers. The cypress-lined Panasoffkee Creek at the southern tip of the lake is tannin-stained, requiring less stealth, but it is so narrow in spots, a canoe is more suitable for this water than a bass boat.

The waters dump into the Withlacoochee River via the Outlet River on the west side of the lake at a wide spot called Princess Lake. Jumper Creek, a couple miles west of the lake and just upstream on the Withlacoochee, and the Dead River area off the Outlet River, are also good. Both waterways are packed with dense vegetation and largemouth. One of my best trips to the lake resulted in the majority of the bass coming from the small creeks.

If beautiful scenery is part of your goals on a fishing trip, the 20-mile-long Jumper Creek should draw your attention. The creek, sometimes only a couple of boat widths wide, is tough to fish due to the overhanging tree limbs, but it is rich in fish due to the water coming from the sand hills and through a swamp. It quickly falls about 44 feet in elevation, according to area locals.

Another great bass trip resulting in a catch (and release) of almost two dozen sizable bass was on the main lake. The late afternoon catch in an area between Shell Point and Coleman's Landing was not exceptional for this lake. One local resort owner caught 30 bass over eight pounds one August, and he just fished two hours each evening right before the sun sank into the horizon. Other good areas lie off Grassy Point, the Yellow Water Creek entrance and the boat trails on the southern end of the lake.

Low light is an ideal time to fish these clear waters, and long rods and thin diameter lines are also best suited for Panasoffkee. As the sky darkens, the line size can increase, say from 10 pound test to 17. Remember that the lake record here reportedly exceeds 16 pounds, and another over 16 was taken just a few years ago. Others of that stature still swim in these waters.

Weedless fare, such as swimming worms, spoons and plastic jerk worms, do well. So do hard minnow-type jerkbaits and small topwater lures fished around and over the submergent vegetation. One rig that is very effective on these waters is the "Wacky" worm rig. It's a belly-hooked, straight-tail plastic worm that is twitched over hydrilla that has grown to about two foot below the surface.

Trolling wild shiners is also an effective way to catch the lake's monster bass. With the shallow cover everywhere, just drop the boat in and start fishing. Most of the lake's resorts and launch areas are on the western shoreline in the village of Panasoffkee.

Not far away is another Sumter County lake that is even less pressured. The 418-acre Lake Miona located off highway 472 offers good bass fishing during the spring and fall months. Check out all the waters around the town of Wildwood for some wild action that most of the state's visitors drive right by!

APPENDICES

APPENDIX A

CENTRAL FLORIDA WATER BODIES & ACREAGE

Citrus County
Lake Bradley 590
Chassohowitzka River 1,000
Crystal River 1,650
Halls River 100
Homosassa River 800
Lake Rousseau 4,000
Lake Tsala Apopka 19,111
Withlacoochee River 3,600

Flagler County
Dead Lake 398
Lake Disston 1,844

Hernando County
Lake Hunter 302
Lake Lindsey 137
Little Withlacoochee River 20
McKethan Lake 57
Mountain Lake 127
Weeki Wachee River 60

Hillsborough County
Alafia River 371
Ed Medard Reservoir
    (Pleasant Grove) 647
Hillsborough River 800
Little Manatee River 150
Pemberton Creek 50
Tampa Bypass Canal 421
Lake Thonotosassa 819
Lake Weeks 55

Lake County
Apopka Beauclair Canal 49
Beakman Lake 94
Lake Beauclair 396
Crescent Lake 143
Lake Denham 269
Lake Dina 62
Lake Dora 4,475
Lake Dorr 1,533

Ella Lake 467
Lake Emma 175
Lake Eustis 7,806
Grasshopper Lake 213
Lake Griffin 16,505
Haines Creek 780
Lake Harris 13,788
Helena Run 38
Lake Hiawatha 48
Holly Lake 98
Lake Hunt 58
Little Lake Harris 2,739
Lake Louisa 3,364
Lake Lucy 335
Lake Minnehaha 2,261
Lake Minneola 1,888
Palatlakaha River 672
Palatlakaha Lake 101
Sellers Lake 1,050
Lake Stewart 64
Lake Susan 81
Lake Umatilla 161
Wildcat Lake 232
Lake Wilson 32
Lake Winona 75
Lake Yale 4,042

Marion County
Lake Bryant 767
Lake Delaney 382
Lake Eaton 307
Half Moon Lake 340
Lake Jumper 305
Lake Kerr 2,830
Lake Lou 130
Mill Dam Lake 210
Oklawaha River 297
Rainbow River 150
Redwater Lake 177
Salt Springs Run 50
Lake Warner (L. Lake Kerr) 695
Lake Weir 5,685

Orange County

Lake Apopka	30,671
Lake Baldwin	196
Lake Barton/Whippoorwill	326
Lake Blanche	121
Lake Butler	1,665
Lake Carlton	382
Lake Chase	135
City of Orlando	819
Clear Lake	339
Lake Conway	1,767
Lake Down	872
Lake Estelle	50
Lake Fairview	401
Lake Gatlin	63
Lake Hart	1,850
Lake Ivanhoe	125
Lake Jessamine	306
Johns Lake	2,417
Lake Lawne	156
Little Fish Lake	23
Lake Louise	145
Lake Maitland	451
Lake Mann	244
Lake Mary Jane	1,158
Lake Minnehaha	96
Lake Mizell	62
Orange County WMD	800
Lake Osceola	157
Lake Palmer	56
Pocket Lake	126
Rock Spring Run	60
Lake Rowena	57
Lake Sheen	565
Starke Lake	203
Lake Sue	140
Lake Susannah	76
Lake Tibet	1,198
Lake Underhill	147
Lake Virginia	223
Wauseon Bay	138
Wekiva River	345

Pasco County

Anclote River	200
Crews Lake	693
Moon Lake	99
Pithlachascotte River	790

Pinellas County

Alligator Lake	72
Chantouqua Lake	44
City of Clearwater	115
City of Dunedin	120
City of St. Petersburg	304
Lake Maggiore	380
Pinellas County APC	304
Sawgrass Lake	47
Lake Seminole	716
Lake Tarpon	2,534
Taylor Park	47
Walsingham Reservoir	80

Putnam County

Cowpen Lake	584
Crescent Lake	15,960
Cross Florida Barge Canal	75
Dunns Creek	72
Georges Lake	816
Little Lake George	1,416
Moss Lee Lake	129
Rodman Reservoir	5,280
Lake Stella	308

Seminole County

Lake Jessup	10,011
Little Wekiva River	100
Puzzle Lake	1,300

Sumter County

Black Lake	245
Lake Deaton	778
Lake Gant	150
Lake Miona	418
Lake Okahumpka	670
Lake Panasoffkee	4,460

Volusia County

Lake Ashby	1,030
Lake Beresford	800
Blue Lake	62
Lake Dexter	1,902
Lake Dias	711
Lake George	46,000
Lake Gleason	91
Gopher Slough	1,088
Lake Harney	6,058
Lake Mcgarrity	107
Lake Monroe	9,406
Mud Lake	304
Nelson Springs Run	150
North Lake Talmadge	121
South Lake Talmadge	60
Spring Garden Lake	521
Lake Woodruf	2,200

APPENDIX B

CENTRAL FLORIDA COUNTY CHAMBERS OF COMMERCE

Citrus County
P.O. Box 1397
Chiefland, FL 32626
904/726-2801

Flagler County
2 Airport Rd.
Star Route Box 18-N
Bunnell, FL 32110

Hernando County
101 East Ft. Dade Ave.
Brooksville, FL 34601
904/796-2420

Hillsborough County/Tampa CVB
111 Madison St. #1010
Tampa, FL 33602
800/826-8358

Lake County
P.O. Box 774
Sorrento, FL 32776
904/383-8801

Marion County
P.O. Box 11206
Ocala, FL 32673
904/347-3434

Orange County (East)
P.O. Box 27027
Orlando, FL 32867
407/277-5951

Orange County (West)
P.O. Box 522
Winter Garden, FL 32787
407/656-1304

Pasco County
407 W. Main St.
New Port Richey, FL 34652
813/842-7651

Pinellas County/Suncoast CVB
4625 East Bay Dr. #109
Clearwater, FL 34624
813/530-6452

Putnam County
P.O. Box 550
Palatka, FL 32178
904/328-1503

Seminole County
P.O. Box 150784
Altamonte Springs, FL 32715
407/834-4404

Sumter County
P.O. Box 550
Bushnell, FL 33513
904/793-3099

Volusia County
P.O. Box 2475
Daytona Beach, FL 32115
904/255-0981

Florida Game and Fresh Water Fish Commission, Central Region, 1239 SW 10th St., Ocala, Florida 32674 or phone (904) 629-8162.

U.S. Forest Service, P.O. Box 13549, Tallahassee, FL 32308.

FISHING & HUNTING RESOURCE DIRECTORY

If you are interested in more productive fishing and hunting trips, then this info is for you!

Larsen's Outdoor Publishing is the publisher of several quality Outdoor Libraries - all informational-type books that focus on how and where to catch America's most popular sport fish, hunt America's most popular big game or travel to productive or exciting destinations.

The perfect-bound, soft-cover books include numerous illustrative graphics, line drawings, maps and photographs. The BASS SERIES LIBRARY and the two HUNTING LIBRARIES are nationwide in scope. The INSHORE SERIES covers coastal areas from Texas to Maryland and foreign waters. The OUTDOOR TRAVEL SERIES covers the most popular fishing and diving destinations in the world. The BASS WATERS SERIES focuses on the top lakes and rivers in the nation's most visited largemouth bass fishing state.

All series appeal to outdoorsmen/readers of all skill levels. The unique four-color cover design, interior layout, quality, information content and economical price makes these books hot sellers in the marketplace. Best of all, you can learn to be more successful in your outdoor endeavors!!

THE BASS SERIES LIBRARY
by Larry Larsen

1. **FOLLOW THE FORAGE FOR BETTER BASS ANGLING VOL. 1 BASS/PREY RELATIONSHIP**
   Learn how to determine the dominant forage in a body of water, and you will consistently catch more and larger bass. Whether you fish artificial lures or live bait, your bass stringer will benefit!

2. **FOLLOW THE FORAGE FOR BETTER BASS ANGLING VOL. 2 TECHNIQUES**
   Learn why one lure or bait is more successful than others and how to use each lure under varying conditions. You will also learn highly productive patterns that will catch bass under most circumstances!

3. **BASS PRO STRATEGIES**
   Professional fishermen know how changes in pH, water temperature, color and fluctuations affect bass fishing, and they know how to adapt to weather and topographical variations. Learn from their experience. Your productivity will improve after spending a few hours with this compilation of tactics!

4. **BASS LURES - TRICKS & TECHNIQUES**
   When bass become accustomed to the same artificials and presentations seen over and over again, they become harder to catch. Learn how to rig or modify your lures and develop specific presentation and retrieve methods to spark or renew the interest of largemouth!

5. **SHALLOW WATER BASS**
   Bass spend 90% of their time in the shallows, and you spend the majority of the time fishing for them in waters less than 15 feet deep. Learn specific productive tactics that you can apply to fishing in marshes, estuaries, reservoirs, lakes, creeks and small ponds. You'll likely triple your results!

THE BASS SERIES LIBRARY

by Larry Larsen

6. BASS FISHING FACTS

Learn why and how bass behave during pre- and post-spawn, how they utilize their senses and how they respond to their environment, and you'll increase your bass angling success! This angler's guide to the lifestyles and behavior of the black bass is a reference source never before compiled. It examines how bass utilize their senses to feed. By applying this knowledge, your productivity will increase for largemouth as well as Redeye, Suwannee, Spotted and other bass species.

7. TROPHY BASS

If you're more interested in wrestling with one or two monster largemouth than with a "panfull" of yearlings, then learn what techniques and habitats will improve your chances. This book takes a look at geographical areas and waters that offer better opportunities to catch giant bass, as well as proven methods and tactics for both man made and natural waters. The "how to" information was gleaned from professional guides and other experienced trophy bass hunters.

8. ANGLER'S GUIDE TO BASS PATTERNS

Catch bass every time out by learning how to develop a productive pattern quickly and effectively. Learn the most effective combination of lures, methods and places. Understanding bass movement and activity and the most appropriate and effective techniques to employ will add many pounds of enjoyment to the sport of bass fishing.

9. BASS GUIDE TIPS

Learn the most productive methods of top bass fishing guides in the country and secret techniques known only in a certain region or state that may work in your waters. Special features include shiners, sunfish kites & flies; flippin, pitchin' & dead stickin' rattlin; skippin' & jerk baits; moving, deep, hot & cold waters; fronts, high winds & rain. New approaches for bass angling success!

INSHORE SERIES
by Frank Sargeant

IL1. THE SNOOK BOOK
"Must" reading for anyone who loves the pursuit of this unique sub-tropic species. Every aspect of how you can find and catch big snook is covered, in all seasons and all waters where snook are found.

IL2. THE REDFISH BOOK
Packed with expertise from the nation's leading redfish anglers and guides, this book covers every aspect of finding and fooling giant reds. You'll learn secret techniques revealed for the first time.

IL3. THE TARPON BOOK
Find and catch the wily "silver king" along the Gulf Coast, north through the mid-Atlantic, and south along Central and South American coastlines. Numerous experts share their most productive techniques.

IL4. THE TROUT BOOK - *COMING SOON!*
You'll learn the best seasons, techniques and lures in this comprehensive book.

OUTDOOR TRAVEL SERIES
by Timothy O'Keefe and Larry Larsen

A candid guide with inside information on the best charters, time of the year, and other vital recommendations that can make your next fishing and/or diving trip much more enjoyable.

OT1. FISH & DIVE THE CARIBBEAN - Volume 1
Northern Caribbean, including Cozumel, Caymans Bahamas, Virgin Islands and other popular destinations.

OT2. FISH & DIVE THE CARIBBEAN - Volume 2 - *COMING SOON!* Southern Caribbean, including Guadeloupe, Bonaire, Costa Rica, Venezuela and other destinations.

DEER HUNTING LIBRARY

by John E. Phillips

DH1. MASTERS' SECRETS OF DEER HUNTING
Increase your deer hunting success significantly by learning from the masters of the sport. New information on tactics and strategies for bagging deer is included in this book, the most comprehensive of its kind.

DH2. THE SCIENCE OF DEER HUNTING - *COMING SOON!*

TURKEY HUNTING LIBRARY

by John E. Phillips

TH1. MASTERS' SECRETS OF TURKEY HUNTING
Masters of the sport have solved some of the most difficult problems you will encounter while hunting wily longbeards with bows, blackpowder guns and shotguns. Learn 10 deadly sins of turkey hunting and what to do if you commit them.

TH2. OUTSMART TOUGH TURKEYS - *COMING SOON!*

BASS WATERS SERIES

by Larry Larsen

Take the guessing game out of your next bass fishing trip. The most productive bass waters in each region of the state are described in this multi-volume series, including boat ramp information, seasonal tactics, water characteristics and much more. Popular and overlooked lakes, rivers, streams, ponds, canals, marshes and estuaries are clearly detailed with numerous maps and drawings.

BW1. GUIDE TO NORTH FLORIDA BASS WATERS
From Orange Lake north and west.

BW2. GUIDE TO CENTRAL FLORIDA BASS WATERS
From Tampa/Orlando to Palatka.

BW3. GUIDE TO SOUTH FLORIDA BASS WATERS
COMING SOON! - from I-4 to the Everglades.

WRITE US!

By the way, if our books have helped you be more productive in your outdoor endeavors, we'd like to hear from you. Let us know which book or series has strongly benefited you and how it has aided your success or enjoyment.

We might be able to use the information in a future book. Such information is also valuable to our planning future titles and expanding on those already available.

Simply write to: Larry Larsen, Publisher, Larsen's Outdoor Publishing, 2640 Elizabeth Place, Lakeland, FL 33813.

We appreciate your comments!

Larry Larsen

Save Money on Your Next Outdoor Book!

Because you've purchased a Larsen's Outdoor Publishing
Book, you can be placed on our growing list of
preferred customers.

● You can receive special discounts on our wide selection
of Bass Fishing, Saltwater Fishing, Hunting, Outdoor
Travel and other economically-priced books written by
our expert authors.

PLUS...

● Receive Substantial Discounts for Multiple Book
Purchases! And...advance notices on upcoming books!

Send in your name TODAY to be added to our mailing list

___ Yes, put my name on your mailing list to receive:

1. Advance notice on **upcoming outdoor books.**
2. Special **discount offers.**

Name_____

Address_____

City/State/Zip_____

**Send to: Larsen's Outdoor Publishing, Special Offers,
2640 Elizabeth Place, Lakeland, FL 33813**

LARSEN'S OUTDOOR PUBLISHING
CONVENIENT ORDER FORM
(All Prices Include Postage & Handling)

BASS SERIES LIBRARY - only $11.95 each or $79.95 for autographed set.

_____ 1. Better Bass Angling - Vol. 1- Bass/Prey Interaction
_____ 2. Better Bass Angling - Vol. 2 - Techniques
_____ 3. Bass Pro Strategies
_____ 4. Bass Lures - Tricks & Techniques
_____ 5. Shallow Water Bass
_____ 6. Bass Fishing Facts
_____ 7. Trophy Bass
_____ 8. Angler's Guide to Bass Patterns
_____ 9. Bass Guide Tips

> **BIG SAVINGS!**
> Order 1 book, discount 5%
> 2 -3 books, discount 10%.
> 4 or more books discount 20%.

INSHORE SERIES - only $11.95 each

_____ IL1. The Snook Book
_____ IL2. The Redfish Book
_____ IL3. The Tarpon Book

DEER HUNTING SERIES - only $11.95 each

_____ DH1. Masters' Secrets of Deer Hunting

TURKEY HUNTING SERIES - only $11.95 each

_____ TH1. Masters' Secrets of Turkey Hunting

OUTDOOR TRAVEL SERIES - only $13.95 each

_____ OT1. Fish & Dive the Caribbean Vol 1 - Northern Caribbean

BASS WATERS SERIES - only $14.95 each

_____ BW1. Guide To North Florida Bass Waters
_____ BW2. Guide To Central Florida Bass Waters

NAME _____

ADDRESS _____

CITY_____STATE_____ZIP_____

No. of books ordered _____ x $_____ each = _____
No. of books ordered _____ x $_____ each = _____
                          Discount   = _____

TOTAL ENCLOSED (Check or Money Order) $_____

Copy this page and mail to:
Larsen's Outdoor Publishing, Dept. RD91
2640 Elizabeth Place, Lakeland, FL 33813

INDEX

D

E

F

G

H

189

191